MODERN MAN
READS THE OLD TESTAMENT

A. Stephan Hopkinson

•

MODERN MAN
READS THE
OLD TESTAMENT

Association Press: New York

TO

JENNIFER ANN

First published in the United States in 1966 by
Association Press, 291 Broadway, New York,
N.Y. 10007

Publisher's Stock Number 1584

Library of Congress Catalog Card Number 65-21963

CONTENTS

HISTORICAL NOTE

MUCH of the Old Testament is occupied with reports — or anticipations — or retrospects — of war. Since war was as much a part of the life of developing nations as fighting is part of the normal activity of a small boy, this is inevitable, but if it is also to be comprehensible, certain facts must be borne in mind. They are as follows:

1. Throughout the period, the major power to the south of Israel is Egypt. She reaches out invading tentacles and on occasion pushes her frontiers right across the whole land of Palestine. Twice she is successfully counter-attacked — but she is the one power who provides a constant influence from beginning to end of recorded Jewish history.

2. Immediately north of Palestine is Syria, a country of approximately equal military strength, with whom the Northern Kingdom — "Israel" — was off and on at war until the fall of Damascus, the capital of Syria, in 732 B.C.

3. In the south of Palestine are the Five Cities of the Philistines, sea-people from Europe and notable warriors: to its south-east and east are Edomites, Moabites, Midianites, and other Arab races, some nomadic and others settled as merchants and farmers.

4. North and east from Palestine across the desert are the empires of Assyria (with its capital at Nineveh) and Babylonia (at one time and briefly the Federation of the Chaldeans), with its capital city of Babylon. They are riverside cities whose highway to the Mediterranean, whether for trade or war, crosses Palestine.

5. East of Babylonia is — for part of our period — the nation of Persia. To the north and west, in what is today Turkey, a succession of races established their dynasties, from the Hittites to the Medes. Still farther north, beside the Black Sea, lived the wild Scythians, horsemen and archers.

9

6. From 1250 B.C. onwards, the twelve tribes of the Hebrews are gradually filtering and fighting their way into Palestine west of the Jordan — some, in fact, never quite get there and settle to the north-east of the river. They form a more or less united nation until 932 B.C., when Solomon's successor, Rehoboam, precipitates a revolution. The Northern ten tribes declare their independence and establish their capital in Samaria. The Southerners remain loyal to the Davidic royal line and the city of Jerusalem. Hereafter, North and South are sometimes in alliance, not infrequently at war.

7. None of these various national powers are precisely contemporary. The rise of one usually means the fall of another and the overrunning of its territories. The conquered nation might then become either independent and tribute-paying, or else be directly ruled in the interest of the conqueror by a governor. Occasionally it was either wiped out altogether or carried off into slavery.

How should a modern reader approach and interpret the Bible, and particularly the Old Testament, which for sheer bulk occupies the greater part of it? Answer must depend in the first place on whether or not such a reader is a Christian. Even if he is not, it is suggested that the Bible has not only a relevancy to life but also a coherent and dynamic attitude which makes it valuable reading. It is, after all, an attempt to apply what was not only a national philosophy but also a personal morality to the changing situations of human experience. It is "existential", in the sense that it is concerned with the application of faith to life, just as it is analytical, in its desire to probe to the roots of the situation and to discover the contribution made by each contributing part to a complete whole.

Anyone who is interested in life must therefore find some interest in a series of related books dealing, as their uniting theme, with the question, "What is it all about? What is life *for?*" Such readers have sometimes been put off by what they have felt to be a necessity either to accept or to reject the Bible as a whole, the belief that selective acceptance or criticism is somehow forbidden, that one cannot usefully read it unless one accepts the attitude which it consistently maintains. However, there is no reason why we should not consider the Bible as we would consider any other great literary work: "Is it *true?*" — true, that is, to what we feel and observe about life as we know it. "Does it enlarge our understanding and deepen our compassion — does it make us more interesting and effective people?"

Great fiction does this, after all, no less than history and biography: so do great drama and great poetry. This implies that it is possible, and indeed valuable, to read the Bible as literature, without necessarily making — or accepting — moral judgements about its situations, or admitting its historical accuracy. We tend, subconsciously, to think of its characters as representing "good" and "bad", as though they were two rival football teams forever playing each other. Instead, we are entitled, if we want, to see them all as a mixture of qualities, as people like ourselves, battling with situations and sometimes finding solutions which the hindsight of history later proved false or imperfect.

Nor does the historicity of the narrative inevitably affect its value. Does any reader of *Hamlet* really worry as to whether Shakespeare's knowledge of Danish history is detailed and accurate? His knowledge of the human heart is all that we care about — let dates and details go hang.

We can, therefore, read the Bible just as a great work of art and yet read it with interest, delight, and profit. But it is as well to remember that every work of art has a right to be approached with humility and a sense of inadequacy. To read the Bible as literature is not to read it with patronage.

Now the Christian reader naturally approaches the Bible, and particularly the Old Testament, differently. To him, in the admirable words of the *Report on Doctrine in the Church of England* (published in 1922 and never adequately studied since), it is "the inspired record of a unique revelation. It is the record of the special preparation for Christ . . . its inspiration may consist either in the inspiration of individual authors or in the inspiration of those who selected, interpreted, and used already existing material" (see pp. 28, 34, or the report, first published by S.P.C.K., in 1938).

That is to say, the Christian's first concern is with the *purpose*

11

of the Bible — which he sees as God's revelation. The God as revealed is not himself changing and developing, though man's apprehension of him does so change and develop.

At first the revelation was conditioned by the limits of man's perception : gradually, that increasing perception (as we see it in the prophets) made the revelation increasingly clear, until it could be finally and completely stated in the living Christ, the Word (or "expression") of God made flesh.

But the God of the New Testament is still the God of the Old ; at the transfiguration Moses and Elijah are seen talking to Christ, as to one whom they had always known, even if their understanding of him was partial and limited. It was not God himself therefore who develops and evolves, who grows out of justice into mercy, out of anger into love. It was man who misunderstood, and misinterpreted — or, it is fairer to say, who could only "see through a glass darkly". But it was still the one and eternal God whom he saw, the God who was to become man at Bethlehem and die, in human form, upon the Cross of Calvary. This, then, is the Saviour men should find when they "search the scriptures and discover their witness" ; this is how that Saviour could interpret to the disciples on the Emmaus road "in all the scriptures the things concerning himself" ; how he could later remind his friends that "everything written about me in the law of Moses and the prophets and the psalms must be fulfilled". Not only is the Old Testament for the Christian a book that Jesus knew, loved and quoted ; it is the book to which the whole pattern of his human life and work were consciously and deliberately related. If we would understand more of the deeper currents of his personality and the implications of his sayings, then we are compelled to look for the background of belief from which they flowed and the thought-forms through which they were expressed. For them the Old Testament is our richest and almost our only source.

So far, therefore, from the Old Testament being just one of the records of primitive man's spiritual experience — a collection having no doubt special historical interest for the specialist, but no major significance for the rest of us — it is a part of learning which no one can afford to neglect. Our own history, our art, and our literature, have all been affected by it to a degree no one dare to compute. Our Christian faith is so rooted in it that the uprooting might well kill the flower; our interpretation of everyday life can find in it parallels, warnings, examples, which are serviceable and fascinating both to those who believe and those who do not, to those who see in them human response to a divine initiative and to those who see only the wistful yearnings of the earthbound for a starry dream come true.

It is not the purpose of this book to set the Old Testament against the historical background of the marching centuries, nor yet to wrestle with the problems of textual correction and scholarly elucidation. It tries only to show how to one reader, at least, the Old Testament is a living writing, dealing with problems of real life, and having direct application to the problems of our demanding world of today.

The passages suggested for reading have been chosen not only for their individual interest but because they embody the theme of the book from which they come.

Read in sequence they give a summary of the total content of the Old Testament. The text used throughout is that of the Authorised Version.

1

THE WORM IN THE APPLE

MAN IS AN INQUISITIVE CREATURE. He wants to know "how"—and that is science. He wants to know "why" — and that is philosophy. The Bible begins with the Book of Genesis (which means "beginning"), with a couple whom it calls "Adam" (meaning just "Man") and "Eve" (meaning "Life").

Into their story it weaves the answers to an immense number of questions. We can imagine a child asking them. "Mummy, why don't snakes have legs?" — "Why do I have to wear clothes?" — "Why do brambles have thorns?" But behind them all is the biggest of questions — "Why is life such a mixture of good and bad?" We get this, of course, ourselves all the time. "Why should my wife die at thirty — she never did anyone any harm?" — "Why does God allow war?" — "Why is one child so much more clever than another?" — they all add up to this same point.

Genesis gives an answer. Not a complete one, but at least the beginning of an explanation. God, it says, plans and intends the perfect happiness, not only of mankind, but of all his creation. He puts man in a place of responsibility — he "names" the animals. And there is at least an anticipation of evolution in the idea that man appears upon the scene after the rest of living things! He represents the sixth phase, or "day", of creation.

God gives man, also, the dangerous gift of freedom. He has power to choose that which is contrary to the will of God. Now if God is perfection, then his will is perfect good. To differ from it is to choose imperfection, the less-than-good. That which is less than good is already evil. So God, giving man freedom, allows the possibility of evil. And man takes the chance, he decides to do what he knows is not the will of God. The thing which he chooses, symbolised as a fruit, is "experience" — knowledge of evil as well as of good.

In the light of experience, the first humans become aware of the possibility of corruption. They see that good can be perverted into evil, and that even the gift of sex, the power "to be fruitful and multiply", to rejoice in the delight of each other's body, can be turned into exploitation, cruelty and jealousy. Instead of the shared rapture of true lovers in one another's arms, they anticipate the shadowy form at the street corner, the mauling of the unsuspecting child. "They knew they were naked" — and so they were afraid. This self-consciousness, this awareness of potential evil, makes them hide from God. They add fear to disobedience, and a moment later add blame of someone else to fear. Not only are husband and wife set on betraying each other, but they add hostility to the animal world to their mutual distrust. And on top of all this, and as its natural sequel, earth itself turns against the people who have betrayed it. They used living things wrongly when they picked a fruit that should have been left to itself. Those who misuse the gifts of earth suffer for it — as the dust-bowls, the eroded valleys and the deserts where once were forests remind us.

But one question is dodged. Why did the serpent cause all the trouble? He is not, in this passage, identified with the devil. He's only more "subtil" than any other creature. He is, in fact, a too-clever-by-half sea-lawyer character. Notice that he doesn't risk eating the fruit himself. He just persuades someone else into it. He's the kind of adolescent who murmurs "Chicken?" — the Iago who plants the poisoned suggestion. Is it power he wants? or the sheer pleasure of destruction? or to score off God? Yet to call him a nasty piece-of-work is to suggest that he was made that way. And who made him? This story doesn't really answer the question as to when evil began : but it does show us the way in which one wrong use of freedom involves every sort of tragic result — and it suggests that freedom to sin ourselves inevitably involves a worse sort of wrong-doing — the power of corrupting others.

2

BLOODY MURDER

WE GET VERY CROSS ABOUT THE frequency of violence upon our T.V. screens — yet we buy more books, see more plays about murder than about any other subject — except, possibly, illicit love.

Why? Probably because death is so very final. It ends all argument. It deprives us of the possibility of come-back. So, because on the whole we all want to live, we are all against the murderer and anxious to see him brought to justice. If he were not to be arrested, perhaps we should be the next victim? A disagreeable thought.

But, to the murderer, this finality must be part of the attraction. I will for ever silence the blackmailing pen, the nagging voice. I will remove from my path my successful rival or dangerous competitor. I will make certain of the legacy, give the enemy his long quietus. I will kill — if I can. Egoism is part of murder, and so is pride. Murderers do not expect to be caught — though no one, indeed, knows how often or how seldom they are. A successful murder, said Dorothy Sayers, is like a successful marriage. It never comes into court. What went wrong with the vegetarian Cain? He is, perhaps, the symbol of settled man, tiller of the soil, dweller in houses. But he has to share the world with Abel — the nomad, the traveller, the man of adventure. And he doesn't like it. He's anxious and he feels himself "put upon", a second-rater.

God — truth, reality, his conscience, if you like — tries to help him see sense. "Be yourself, boy. Be true to your own self, and it'll come all right. If you once let these ideas into your mind, they'll grow on you and you'll never get rid of them." But he does let them in, and the row blazes up, as so many rows do, with hot words passing into hotter deeds, till a man is dead —

17

hidden, it would seem, below the ground hugger-mugger.

Murder is followed by lying, by all that miserable business of falsehood which is part of the horror of the crime. With it comes a sneer that echoes down through history — "Am I my brother's keeper?" Though he die of hunger in India, be machine-gunned in South Africa, jailed in Hungary, unemployed on Tyneside, unvisited in the house next door, it's still no business of mine.

Murder may be spawned of hatred and envy and nourished in anger, but there's a kind of death-in-the-heart amongst us, a matter of no-caring, which leads to death-on-the-road or death-in-the-back-street.

"Thou shalt not kill — but need'st not strive. Officiously to keep alive."

GENESIS 7

3

WATER, WATER, EVERYWHERE...

PSYCHOLOGISTS ASSURE US THAT the concept of water, the great sea that sometimes washes through our dreams, symbolises the subconscious. To the Jew it certainly symbolised the chaotic and unreasonable, the threatening power which could overwhelm, the place where strange monsters lived.

Now that power had once, they believed (and not they only but many of our forefathers, from Babylonians to Greeks with their tales of Atlantis), almost destroyed mankind. Because they were wholeheartedly God-centred, and saw the divine activity in all that happened, they explained this destruction in terms of divine anger at man's stubborn wickedness.

Yet the story, as they told it, is one of pruning rather than of uprooting. Breeding couples are to be preserved of every living thing that exists, good and bad. How well, we feel, the company of the mosquito and hyena might have been avoided. But man is not, even at this stage, allowed to dodge his responsibility for the preservation of life. He has to transport the beasts, birds and insects, and to feed them as well.

We, in our day of broiler batteries and fattened calves, may in theory recognise the fact of evolution and of our kinship with the beasts. Yet we use it to exploit and destroy them. The great herds of buffalo are gone, and the whales are following them. Africa is losing the animals that were its glory: the birds live on, but in cage rather than in copse. Perhaps our fondness for cat and dog, the revival of riding on horses amongst the most industrial of our city dwellers, is a wistful recognition of a kinship that was once very precious. It is thousands of years since last we "tamed" a new animal species and made them our friends, though some say the porpoise and the dolphin are learning to understand our ways. But here, at the beginning of time, man and beast are one, almost as they were in the legend of the centaur. Man uses his opposed thumb and technique of tools to build a ship, but he sends out the dove to report on the world across the waters. And it is sad that the rainbow, token in the story of God's covenant with man as to the steadfast succession of the seasons, should look down upon the end of this fellowship, when "the fear of you and the dread of you shall be upon every beast of the earth".

We have lost our kinship with the beasts, and so we mistrust the animal aspect of our compound nature. Because we mistrust it, we fight it. And sometimes it wins, so that we turn back the pages and become ourselves tiger, monkey, crocodile — or just plain donkey or fluttering hen. Sometimes the rational side of us wins, and we become withered, bloodless, dead sticks, not living beings.

But we *are* animals still, lineal descendants of the apes, kith and kin to all other creatures, and we need to accept this fact of our nature, if we are to grow onwards and upwards. Because the saints are holy, in the sense that they are whole, complete, developed people, they are aware of the wholeness and unity of life: again and again the stories about them remind us of their comprehension and love for the lesser children of God. Jerome and his lion, Francis with the birds, Cuthbert and the otter — there is no fear, but a mutual love and a mutual respect. And if we reject the evidence of the saints, there is still the evidence of physiology. Each human embryo, we are told, passes before birth through those stages of actual physical evolution which have taken our race millions of years to span. We carry, each of us, in ourselves, our own Ark.

GENESIS II. 1–9

4

SKY-SCRAPING

THE BEDOUIN ISRAELITES MUST have been as puzzled by the ruins of lost civilisations as they were impressed by the accomplishments of existing ones. Why and how could people of such ability have been destroyed? They stood agape, as tourists do to this day in Chichen-Itza or Angkor-Wat, in Pompeii and Palmyra — as perhaps they will tomorrow in Manhattan, Manchester and Moscow.

And they explained the death of the cities as due to two things — to pride, and to internal division. We should probably add some economic causes: the gradual impoverishment of the soil around the areas of dense population, the development of disease, the changing pattern of commerce.

But to those who saw a moral responsibility in every situation, who believed that the choice between right and wrong is always confronting us anew, the issues were rather clearer — nor is their diagnosis necessarily a false one.

Men, they said, excited by their technical ability, decided they had no more place for God and that they could take over his functions. The tower they set out to build is an expression of this. Instead of the initiative being with God, who comes to man, yet is always greater than man, and therefore must always be beyond man's complete comprehension, the initiative shall be with man himself. He will now enthrone himself in heaven, and reorganise affairs to suit his own ideas. He has the resources — bricks of baked clay, mortar of seepage bitumen — and he has the technical know-how.

The attempt failed : it still fails. And it failed on that first occasion because the builders were so sure of themselves that they omitted to take into account the full facts of the situation. They were typical of that bureaucratic mind which over-simplifies, reducing every situation from its potent reality to fit in with the organisation scheme. They refused to recognise essential *difference* and variety in mankind, and tried to compel all into uniformity.

So life rejected them — as it has a way of doing. The differences between men blaze up into a destroying fire. "They didn't speak each other's language" : the very fact of their proximity to each other intensified their differences rather than fusing them together.

This is always the danger of community. Unless we are determined to *love* our neighbour, we are apt to hate him. The foreigner who is all right as long as I only experience him at second-hand through books and films, smells of garlic when he lives next door, sings too loudly, observes curious feasts and fasts. Not even a common purpose will unite us for long. How many alliances, wise and essential alliances, scarcely last the length of the war which creates them — how few survive into the peace that follows. Age after age our dreaming cities rise, only to topple when they cease to be a focus of good-will and a symbol of shared purpose, but become instead a tyrant's fortress or the scene of fratricidal hate.

A great common purpose demands of its participants greatness of soul — it does not, necessarily, impart it. The better the plan, the nobler the political concept, the better and nobler people it needs if it is to be implemented. Good laws do not make men good : they demand goodness in those who are to practise them. It is often better to be content with short-term planning and half-way good — which can be realised — rather than to make attempt upon the magnificent but hopeless. This, at least, is true of politics, itself "the art of the possible" ; — and politics is a microcosm of human relationships.

5

PIONEER AND PILGRIM

WE MISUSE THE WORD "UNIQUE", softening it down until it means no more than "slightly uncommon", so that we speak of "a unique bargain" when we merely mean that a product is rather cheaper than usual.

But now and then something happens which is entirely out on its own, an event which is a landmark in history, a person who seems representative of a different race cast in a nobler mould.

In this sense, Abraham is unique, and is reverenced as such by three great religions. He is one of the great "originals", the men and women who really do start something. In his case, what was started is all that is implied in the words "religious reformation". He is the ancestor of Paul and Luther and Knox and Wesley.

For Abraham "goes out from his father's house". We are told that in the ancient city of Ur they worshipped a moon goddess, and that within its walls all dwelt under her protection. Abraham, then, dares to break with all patterns of security — the "establishment" of his day — to go and look for new truth in new places.

He is "called" — as every pioneer is called — to "something lost beyond the ranges, something waiting for you". But he is free to do what most of us do, and to shut his ears to the voice. After all, to answer it means giving up many of the things which other people value most highly. It means buying a pig in a poke, it's spending everything on a treasure-hunt — which may not pay off. It means showing a quality which is common to inventors and pioneers and reformers and other people of vision — and is very rare in the rest of us, the willingness to sacrifice solid quality for shadow; to see that the good can be the enemy of the better; that common-sense seldom carries us beyond the harbour mouth.

But Abraham *goes,* and by going out and going alone he becomes the "father of many nations", the pioneer whose pilgrim road uncounted others will follow. He involves himself in a dangerous life of hard choice and desperate adventure, where his only hope is in the guiding spirit of his god, a god whom as yet he hardly knows.

The city of Ur, where most of us live, was called by Bunyan — another pilgrim —the city of *Despair*. So it may be, for those who are dreaming of a better — though they do not know where to look for it and sometimes try to find it in the various forms of forgetfulness which drugs or even death can offer. But to others it is *Vanity Fair,* the city which offers immediate satisfactions and competing delights, the city which has its own form of comfortable religion to hallow its activities.

The time comes when the trumpet sounds or the postman knocks, when the ship waits and the chance offers. But the way is dangerous and the destination uncertain. So we draw the curtains, turn up the television, and congratulate ourselves on our common-sense.

Yet something deep within us protests, suggesting that we've missed our chance and failed our better self. We reply by rationalising that failure, sneering at the fool who suggested departure, at the rash friend who is still planning to go. To silence the nagging voice within, we condemn the pioneer outside — and once we've agreed to condemn him, it's not so very hard to put him to death. Prophet and visionary, pilgrim or reformer, better he die than that we be disquieted.

GENESIS 19. 1–30

6

FIRE, BRIMSTONE, AND SODIUM CHLORIDE

ALL THAT MOST OF US KNOW about Lot is that his wife became a pillar of salt. Yet this is the least important part of the story. Maybe, like those pathetic figures to be seen in the museums of Naples, she was calcified by volcanic dust, as she turned back to look for her valuables: maybe some solitary rock overlooking the Dead Sea desolation

23

bore a curious resemblance to a human shape and so was given an appropriate name (we all know of similar rocks ourselves).

But the story of Lot is also the story of Abraham, whose nephew he was and whose companion he had become. The partnership did not last. Ultimately they found that pasture-shortage made separation advisable, and Abraham very generously offered the younger and more active man first choice of territory. He chose the good grasslands of Jordan, and set up his tents near the twin cities of Sodom and Gomorrah.

This brought immediate trouble. The wealthy cities in their comfortable valley were, in the course of local wars, raided by a confederacy of petty kings — and Lot was captured with all his goods.

Then follows (chapter 14) a fine story of desert fighting, of blood-loyalty, of Bedouin hospitality, and Bedouin pride. Through it there moves the strange remote figure of the priest-King Melchisedec, in whom early Christian commentators saw a foreshadowing or "archetype" of Christ himself. Lot, rescued from captivity, goes back to Sodom amongst its oil-seepages, disregarding warnings of disaster as so many dwellers on volcano-slopes have always disregarded them. Then follows earthquake, eruption, and — it seems — the ignition of petroleum gas. Not only are the cities wiped out, but the whole geography of the neighbourhood is altered — as occurred, thousands of years after, at Krakatoa, Sodom and Gomorrah become symbols of desolation. But they became also symbols of sin, a sin described at some length in chapter 19, a sin which has taken its name from Sodom itself (though Judges 19 records a similar sort of story from Gibeah in the tribal zone of Benjamin).

Now to the original writers and readers of the Old Testament, the sin of Sodom was so hideous (although so frequent in the ancient world as to be used by St. Paul in Romans 1 as evidence of general pagan corruption) that they looked at the furnace of the Dead Sea Valley and saw in it the punishment for man's misdoings. But to us perhaps the grimmest passage in a grim story is verse 8, suggesting as it does an attitude to women which subordinates their integrity and chastity entirely to the responsibility of hospitality. Lot is quite prepared to throw both his

24

young daughters to the ravening mob, in order to preserve his guests. He accepts a code which puts the safety of the stranger under his roof before that of his own family. Even if we allow this a sort of nobility, one would surely have preferred to see him fighting for his friends rather than trying to buy off their lives with his daughters' honour. Not that the unhappy daughters themselves had a very strong idea of chastity, to judge by the incident in verses 30 to 38 — an incident recorded to explain racial kinship with the hated tribes of Moab and Ammon, whilst at the same time scoring at their expense.

And Lot himself, the man for the easy way, the nomad so softened by city life that he's afraid of the hills of home (verse 19), is really a contemptible figure.

What is interesting, however, about the story is the recognition of that problem which later confronted Christ himself, the problem of the suffering of the innocent. The whole last section of chapter 18 is an assertion that God does *not* involve the innocent in the consequence of another's guilt — an assertion that we cannot, on our own experience, possibly accept. Yet it is a gallant effort to maintain both the power and the justice of God : to accept both his universal activity and his no less universal benevolence. We, on our part, see in this common involvement of men part of the pattern of the divine purpose, a recognition of our unbreakable kinship with each other — and of our individual and corporate responsibility for each other as a result. Yet we can admire the determination of those who, long ago, reflecting upon the Dead Sea disaster, could maintain that even in that grim holocaust, justice was meted out and the righteous (or in Lot's case, the very moderately righteous) were preserved.

GENESIS 22. 1–19

7

FINAL DEMAND

WHY DO WE WRITE OUR NAMES in visitors' books (if well behaved), scribble them on walls (if less-so)? Why are we so anxious, departing, to leave behind us footsteps on the sands of time? Is it because we fear the sheer insignificance of our life and long somehow to be perpetuated, even if it is only by a massive marble slab in a forgotten corner of the cemetery? Are we attracted to anything which may prolong our name here on earth when we have passed from it?

Of course, children are a more abiding memorial. We live again in our posterity, a fact of which the Jews have always been particularly conscious. Perhaps no other race has ever been so aware of the importance of the family structure, unless it be the Chinese. And, to the Jews as to the Chinese, it was sons who mattered most. No man need feel he died a failure if he left a worthy son behind him.

Now to Abraham had been granted an extraordinary and most precious privilege. In extreme old age — there's no need to argue about the exactness of this as recorded, but at least at a surprising age — his wife had borne a son. Naturally, he was his father's delight and treasure — indeed, his subsequent weakness of character suggests that he was much over-protected in childhood.

But, one day, his father is visited with a horrible thought. Can it be that he loves this child *too much*? If it came to the choice would he actually love him more than God himself?

To a man whose whole life had been spent in the loyal service of an ideal — his God — the thought was quite appalling. Day and night it haunted him — and it had about it a fearful truth. (He did, in fact, love his son "too much" in the sense that he loved him in the wrong sort of way, as an extension of himself and not as an individual, as the channel through which he — the man Abraham — would be perpetuated as a nation, and not as a human-being in his own right.)

How can he possibly prove to himself that he's wrong, and root out from his heart what he comes to see as a temptation? An answer suggests itself. He must give the son to God. He will hand over his child, Isaac, entirely to God, through the bitter road of "sacrifice". The very word "sacrifice" literally means to "make holy", to "dedicate". So the life of Isaac shall be dedicated to the God who gave it. Then follows that sad journey, to

26

a hilltop (near to the sky where God lives), with its preparations so appalling to the father, so full of unsuspecting interest to the boy. Many a parent taking a child to hospital must have shared the feeling of Abraham and known what "dramatic irony" means when it's experienced at first hand, of the terrifying significance the simplest phrase can bear. "Are we getting late, father?" — "When will I be coming home?"

So his passionate love for God drives Abraham to the verge of murder. He *will* prove that this love is supreme in his heart. There follows a divine intervention. And from this intervention comes the awareness that God is in *both* forms of love, that neither excludes the other, that a man can and must love both his neighbour and his God, that, indeed, God gave him the child in order that it *should* be loved.

The "ram caught in the thicket" may well represent, historically, the substitution of animal for human sacrifice. Over and over again the stories of the Old Testament are crystallisations of history, the focussing in an individual situation of a national experience. The moment came when men saw clearly that it was wrong to kill other men to offer them to the gods, and so learned to use animals instead.

But these stories are also pictures of real human situations, and human situations tend to repeat themselves. The time still comes when love for God may seem to demand sacrifices almost beyond human power to make. And it still happens that those who do try their hardest to meet the demand and grant the sacrifice with a willing heart find that at the last they are spared it, and that unexpected help and escape are granted them.

GENESIS 27

8

JEALOUS TWINS

IT CANNOT TOO OFTEN BE SAID — or written — that the Bible is not the story of saints, but of human beings, some of whom are trying to be saints. And they are trying in a great variety of circumstances.

Now one of the most difficult of relationships is that of brothers (and sisters) to each other. Our Freudian obsession with parent-child complexes leads us to forget this. So does the much looser fabric of our contemporary life in which brothers, nominally sharing the same home, are absorbed in separate interests and create their own pattern of friendships. But in earlier societies brothers, thrown by circumstances into one another's company and dependent upon one another's good-will, developed powerful emotions towards each other, for good or ill. A significant factor in forming these emotions was the matter of inheritance, and of the way in which family property and hereditary distinction would be transferred and divided. In general, such inheritance proceeded in two entirely different ways, according to the tradition of the society concerned.

First, there is the right of "primogeniture", the claim of the eldest son to succeed his father. In British tradition, he takes his father's title (if any), his estate (ditto), and in all things *becomes* his father. (In some other traditions, the estate is divided between, and the title taken by, *all* the sons.) "Primogeniture" gives stability to society, and has therefore been popular with the conservative-minded : it perpetuates a pattern of society. Where it exists, the younger sons go out to earn their own living; the landed tradition in England was in favour of the services, the professions, or settlement overseas as all quite suitable. The younger sons may resent their elder brother's absolute right, but they accept it — and the implied responsibility to make their own way and their own mark in the world. So far as they inherit a title, it is one which gradually disappears with their descendants, except in those cases where the senior line came to an end and the honours reverted to a junior branch.

But nomadic or wandering — as opposed to settled and agricultural — peoples have a different tradition of inheritance. In their case, the older sons go off with a share of the flocks and herds that are the family inheritance, whilst the *youngest* son remains at home to care for the old people. When a nomadic people settle down on the land, the two traditions clash — and some of the fraternal feuds of Genesis (as in this story, or in that of Joseph and his brothers) seem to refer back to such clashes.

28

For this is a picture of the astute man of affairs defrauding the simple countryman — and it is in some ways an anticipation of that Jewish-Arab feud which continues to this day. We do not have to justify Jacob in any way, or to see his behaviour as anything but extremely sharp practice. What the story does, however, make clear is that Jacob has from the beginning a sense of purpose and a readiness to think and plan (however crookedly) towards his ends.

In comparison, Esau is irresponsible, concerned (see chapter 25, verses 29 to 34) only with the present, and so incapable of becoming the founder of a nation. The elder by a second or two, husband of foreign wives who didn't get on with his parents (see chapter 26, verses 34 and 35), he has by the strong right of primogeniture a claim to succeed his father in authority. That this claim was dishonestly usurped does not alter the fact that he was unworthy to exercise it. The question still remains as to the moment at which the able rival should supplant the rightful holder of a post; when does a Henry overthrow a Richard, a Fletcher Christian maroon a Captain Bligh? Has incompetence a right to undisturbed authority? or may it be forced to surrender a post it is unworthy to hold?

Here, in the strife between Esau and Jacob, is foreshadowed the historic tension between the conservative and the revolutionary, between the man who believes in inherited rights, however poorly employed, and the man who believes that failure to use them properly cancels such rights or leaves them for another to seize.

GENESIS 28. 10–17

9

JACOB AT BETHEL

WE HAVE RECENTLY BEEN blamed for thinking of a God who is "up there" or "out there" rather than "in here". God, we are reminded, is within us. He is part of us — or we are part of him. To think of him, therefore, as someone or something who intervenes from outside is to suggest that he is separate, remote — and that there are parts of life in which he is not at present involved. Instead, we are to look for him everywhere, and to find him at work in the most unexpected places. He will not be limited to church or temple, nor active only in the hearts of the overtly devout. For all men are his children and all life his dominion.

The story of Jacob at Bethel is a case in point. It's the story of a man who, on his way to look for a wife, is caught by nightfall on what Shakespeare would have called a "blasted heath". So he makes a little shelter for himself, against weather and wild animals, out of the loose stones that abound, and lies down in it to sleep.

And in the night he dreams, and sees the sky full of shining messengers of God, coming and going between earth and heaven. The place, so lost and lonely, is as busy as a terminal airport; all about him throngs the ceaseless traffic of eternity.

So he wakes with a new certainty of the purpose of human life and the part he has to play in it, with new faith that God is all about him as he goes on his way to woo.

Now the point of this story surely is that God is here and now, and not that he is up there and far away. Because of our blindness, it implies, we fail to see the ladder "set up to heaven at Charing Cross". But it is there all the same, that world invisible but real, and for all we know its citizens may not be so invisible as we suppose. The word "angel" only means "messenger" — and who can tell what forms the messenger of God may take? After all, a messenger is only a "person who carries a message", and it may be that we are ourselves sometimes called to be angels in just that sense, people who are charged by God with a message to pass on to another. Nor does the message have to be specifically "religious". God's world has an infinite variety, and he is concerned with every single aspect of that multiform variety. His angels may find themselves bearing a wider range of messages than any postman. Yet they are still his messengers, evidence of his care, whether they be human-beings or ministering spirits of another sort.

We see, too, that the angels are going up as well as coming down. This suggests a God who is committed to the situation, a God who would not balk at the total commitment involved in becoming a man himself. Some kinds of religion think in terms of angels coming down, of a God who is authority issuing orders; to others' minds the angels only go up, carrying the desperate prayers of men to a being eternally remote. The God of Jacob is a god whose activity is perpetual and intimate.

GENESIS 32. 13–30

10

WOMEN AND CHILDREN FIRST

WE ALL OF US ADMIRE COURAGE, whether moral or physical. But what exactly do we mean by "courage"? G. K. Chesterton — probably quite wrongly — identified it with the French word *"courir"*, "to run", and in one way courage certainly does mean a charge into danger, a defiance of long odds, a refusal to accept the possibility of defeat.

But there is another sort of courage, which perhaps ought to have a different name. This is realisation that there's no chance at all of success, nor even of survival — and the willingness to go forward, just the same. It's the quiet determination which can calculate risk, yet refuse to be frightened by the result of that calculation.

Now Jacob had no "courage", in the first sense. He's a long-term planner, the ancestor of all back-room boys. He worked seven years for a girl he loved, found himself cheated of her and served a further term in order to win her. Every step in his life was a matter of foresight: he would have made a chess-player of championship class.

And now, as occasionally happens to the calculator, he's come up against tough physical fact. He's likely to be beaten up, by his indignant twin-brother Esau, whom he's already cheated over his inheritance.

31

So he plans a system of cumulative bribes. He divides up the animals that are his portable capital and sends them ahead of him in waves — each designed to wash away some of his brother's prejudice. After his livestock — his family, wives and children. They are expendable, as compared to his own life, though more valuable than his flocks.

But, though a man may run away from reality for much of his life, one day he has to face it. It is the legend of the *"doppelganger"*, the twin-self that haunts us and one day meets us face-to-face, the day we know ourselves as we are and shrink from the knowledge. It is in meeting our true self and coming to terms with ourselves that we become adult persons.

So Jacob, the ingenious schemer, the wideboy who always knew a way round, comes up against reality, the reality of his dark inner self. For some men this meeting is a recognition, the willingness to accept something about themselves they have always tried to deny. Van der Post claims that the white South African, for instance, will always be marred and incomplete until he recognises his need for the black South African, for the inner self which he rejects but must at last accept.

For other men the meeting is a battle, the struggle of the butterfly against the chrysalis, of the thing which will be fighting its way clear of the thing that is. And fight ends in full recognition — in exchanging names with each other. Jacob, the deceiver, is beaten — and he is beaten by Jacob, the child of God.

GENESIS 39

11

HELL HATH NO FURY

JOSEPH WAS THE SORT OF MAN Samuel Smiles most admired. He got on by his own efforts, and in spite of circumstances. He was honest, evidently : attractive, as he found to his cost : extremely hard-working —"whatsoever they did there, he was the doer of it". Add to this a gift for interpreting events, and a patience to wait on them. A thoroughly spoilt childhood was a handicap. Possibly, however, it left him with a sense of destiny, the conviction that everything was, in the end, going his way.

But he found himself in the most difficult of situations — to be wooed by a woman whom he must either refuse, at the cost of her undying hate, or else accept, contrary to all honour.

In the upshot, of course, she waits for a chance when he is alone — tries to seduce him, and then accuses him of attempted rape. The other servants, who are evidently extremely jealous of this handsome young foreigner who has been promoted over all their heads and may well have interfered with some of their small domestic dishonesties, leap at the chance to be rid of him. But now comes the mystery.

If a Louisiana senator, a colonel in the National Guard, learns that his wife has been assaulted by a coloured labourer in her own bedroom, what does he do? Ask for a mild gaol sentence, or reach for his gun?

Here is one of the master-race, whose honour has been challenged — and by a homeless slave, bought in the market. Why not throw him to the crocodiles? Why not indeed — since a slave has no rights? If Potiphar forbears, it must be because he doesn't, in his heart of hearts, believe the story. Maybe he knew — he feared — Joseph was entirely innocent.

What does he *do* in this situation? Can he openly give his wife the lie and leave Joseph in an impossible situation? A worse man would have shut the slave's mouth for ever. But Potiphar is far from being a bad man. So he compromises, covers it all up, gets rid of the slave and tries to forget the whole disagreeable situation.

What would we do ourselves? Here is, on the one hand, loyalty to a person who has major claims upon us, someone who can expect that we shall take their word as to truth, whatever may be the evidence. On the other hand, the stranger, the man outside — who may not be right after all.

It's the problem of the manager, who must decide between the foreman of long standing and the labourer, signed on last

33

week — the headmaster, who suspects the teacher is wrong but prefers to accept his version rather than trust the child's story. We can all of us find ourselves in Potiphar's place, and we may not even have the honesty to compromise, preferring instead to believe in the person we know, to stand by our class, to condemn the stranger with the different accent, to reject dangerous truth. Pilate did this, and there are many Pilates.

But what, one wonders, did Mrs. Potiphar say when, a little later, she was introduced at a palace banquet to the new Grand Vizier and found herself going in to dinner behind his wife?

GENESIS 47. 1–27

12

SPECULATION IN FARM PRICES

IT IS A FACT OF EGYPTIAN history that at one stage the country was under the control of a dynasty of "Shepherd Kings", the Hyksos, and that the rest of the Egyptians bitterly resented the primacy and prosperity of an alien pastoral people settled amongst them. Although there is immense argument as to the date of the Exodus, the Pharaoh under whom it took place, and the exact relationship of Hebrew and Egyptian before and after, that there *was* such a relationship (and an embittered one, leading to final escape or expulsion) there is no doubt.

History, too, has plenty of parallels to the story of Joseph, the man of a *"carrière ouverte aux talents"*, the brilliant foreigner whose intelligence and charm together carry him to the top. Disraeli was one such, if the word "foreigner" be interpreted rather freely.

But what is the first loyalty of the successful careerist? When — as with the Hebrews — family ties are strong, it is exercised toward the family. Joseph begins by importing his own people, and making sure they get the best of everything. Because it's "in the Bible", we accept the propriety of this without question. Yet

34

when it happens in politics, are we equally happy about it? Should a prime minister pack his government with blood relations — on the grounds first, that he can trust them, second, that he owes it to them? Should an American Congressman staff his office with his relations (at government expense)? Or take the case of the oriental civil servant, who makes special concessions to his cousins. Or the African householder who fills the home beyond all sanitary limits with his blood relations to the eighteenth degree. We are quick to condemn "nepotism" when we see it outside our own situation. Yet is there not a link between such nepotism and the acceptance of blood-responsibility? Is our own criticism of it not somewhere related to our anxiety that the state should relieve us of all claims from our indigent relatives?

But, whatever we think of Joseph's loyalty to the family who had once rejected him, how shall we judge his attitude over the famine, of which he had advance information?

What he actually does is to strengthen Pharaoh's hold upon his nation immeasurably, by enabling him to become landlord of his entire country (with the exception of its state-subsidised church). In order to break down traditional local loyalty, the people are moved wholesale from their homes and resettled at royal convenience. Their only portable wealth — their livestock — is "nationalised"; they become, in effect, share-croppers paying a rent-charge in kind and without capital resources.

This is a classic picture of the way in which a free nation of yeoman farmers can become a proletariat — a parallel, perhaps, to our own industrial revolution. It is at least a remarkable example of the way economic pressure determines social structure. And, whilst we must accept the fact that Joseph's loyalty must have existed, as he saw it, towards Pharaoh alone without regard to the ultimate welfare of the Egyptians, how far does this apply in our own life-situations today?

Is a manager *solely* responsible to shareholders, or does he also have a duty (which may conflict with it) to employees? How far is it right to make use of people's necessity for one's own financial advantage? For instance, can one rightly demand inflated prices simply because of scarcity (where no possible rise in cost to oneself need be considered)? Is cornering the market, condemned totally by mediaeval Christendom, now to be accepted as perfectly permissible business practice? Indeed, is any exploitation of other people's need to one's own advantage (or to the profit of the organisation for which one works) in accordance with Christian teaching and belief? Is it morally better — or worse — if it is done in somebody else's name or on their authority, rather than as admitted and unadulterated self-interest? We need a good deal of honest thinking about these matters.

Finally — and in defence of Joseph! — Pharaoh's final rake-off was one-fifth of the total land-yield. In most of our share-cropping schemes — and in pre-revolutionary France — the pro-portion claimed by the owner has been one-third. Matters have deteriorated since the days of Joseph.

EXODUS 2 and 3. 1–15

13

LONELY DESTINY

IT IS NEVER A SAFE THING TO BE a favourite. The person whose affection you possess may die or go away — and then all the jealousy of your companions has full expression. This can happen to racial groups or social classes as well as to individuals. Every revolution has its particular enemies whom it destroys because they belong to a category (or colour, religion, politics, or property) which has been favoured before.

So the Hebrews, living comfortably on their "white high-lands", suddenly find themselves turned into labourers and artisans. What is more, they are subjected to a form of population control. This is not as ferocious as the "genocide" from which the Jews have subsequently suffered, since it is designed to lead to eventual identification rather than extinction. Their girls will marry Egyptians and become absorbed in the national structure. Yet is horrible enough and will eliminate them as an independent group.

Now one Jewish wife (of the priest-tribe of Levi, as was her husband : a clerical family on both sides) shows great determination and resource. She makes use of the maternal instinct of her own sex and succeeds not only in getting her child adopted into the royal family, but in wet-nursing him herself. He grows up, according to Jewish tradition (quoted in Acts 7, verse 22), within the court circle and enjoying all the advantages of education. But somewhere along the line he becomes aware of his birth. He accepts its liabilities and intervenes (though cautiously) on behalf of one of his fellow-countrymen. Word travels instantly along the grape-vine, and someone, perhaps an informer, reports the matter. Moses has to fly for his life to the desert, where his city-polished courtesy and his personal courage (and perhaps his training in weapon drill) win him a Bedouin girl for a wife. He is now an exile twice over. He is thrown out by the clans to whom his education has linked him. And he is not even accepted by the people of his birth.

This is a situation not unlike that of the white South African who takes the side of the black one. One group treats him as a traitor; the other suspects his motives. It is, of course, the position of anyone who is forced to transfer loyalty, however good and sincere his motives. But this total isolation is what gives to Moses his particular strength, since it forces him to dependence upon God. Alone in the desert, he sees an extraordinary sight. God is revealed to him through and in nature — a bush — but nature invested with a new quality. This is that radiance of the divine presence, the "shekinah" as the Jews called it, which is symbolised in Christian artistic tradition by the halo. Fire, the symbol of destruction, is here the sign of presence and protection. It is light without heat, glory without injury.

Notice too the *gradual* unfolding of revelation.

First, the personal call, individually and by name, to take part in a conversation. (Once remarkably expressed in a dramatic reading by a young actor who used the same tone and inflexion of voice for both God and Moses, but made the voice of God much quieter.) Moses is not dragooned into acceptance, but is roused by discussion.

Second, God having made himself known, goes on to identify

himself with the traditional faith of Moses' race. He recalls him
to his national loyalty.

Third, he declares himself concerned in the situation and
intending to take action.

Fourth, he calls on Moses to help him.

(At this stage, Moses breaks in, to protest his incapacity, and
gets his answer that —)

Fifth, not only will God be with him, but he has also a long-
term and continuing purpose for the enterprise.

(Again Moses asks for some evidence he can show of his
authority to lead, and is given it.)

Sixth, the assurance of God's timeless and continuing identity.
He is the eternal present, the God who always is. This will link
the God of history and experience, the God their fathers had
known, with the God of the future, the God who, so many centuries later, still is, and still is active through and behind history,
still aware of oppression, still calling on men and women to go
out and set the people free. Yet he still waits cautiously upon
their co-operation, still refuses to bulldoze them into conformity
with his plans.

Exodus 5

14

LABOUR AGITATION AND STRIKE ACTION

WHAT DOES AN EMPLOYER DO
when two suspiciously well-educated and seemingly self-
appointed demagogues come to him and ask for a special holiday
period for his workers — even if they produce some specious
and superstitious claim that this will help to ward off natural
catastrophe? Clearly, he does his best to discredit these leaders
by making their intervention a reason for toughening up conditions, and depriving the workers of such privileges as he can.
In the case before us, he does it by insisting on a doubling up of
function. Brickmakers must become harvesters into the bargain.

And the people who are hardest hit are the responsible minor officials, the "officers of the children of Israel", who are made to suffer at first-hand so that they will in turn encourage their people to turn on Moses and Aaron. The method is a traditional way, and at first is highly effective. The Hebrews reject the very men who can save them; and are only gradually persuaded to trust them.

What, in similar situations today, do we suppose that unjustly oppressed groups, in industry or elsewhere, are expected to do? Reasonable statement of grievance may be met as it is in this case, not just by blank refusal, but by a calculated policy of victimisation. Such a policy is most successful if it is directed, not against the leaders themselves — whose suffering may add prestige to their cause — but against the lesser lights, the self-sacrificing and responsible, but inconspicuous. In this way, the brave words of leadership seem empty talk, and their position one of privilege rather than peril.

The interesting answer of Exodus, of course, is not that of passive resistance or Gandhi's *"satyagraha"*. It is one of militancy, even if this militant action emanates from God rather than from man. There is, the story suggests, a moment when victimisation and exploitation (the situation of the Hebrews) can only be put right by some form of direct action. And it is, in this case, action which leads to bloodshed: not to mention looting.

Here again, we may protest that this is not a Christian guide to conduct, but simply the historical record of what happened in a given situation. In that case, let us at least read it as a warning to all exploiters and perhaps as an encouragement to the exploited. But these last need to take note that the first steps on the way to liberty may involve set-back and suffering, and that those who will lead them to ultimate freedom may take them by a hard and stony road before they reach it. To suffer from injustice is not necessarily to deserve independence, let alone authority; ill-treated servants seldom make generous and understanding masters. This is not a reason for maintaining them in servitude, but for treating them so well that they will in turn make wise employers and responsible leaders. There is no need to name examples — the world today is full of them.

15

PLAGUES OF EGYPT

ENORMOUS NUMBERS OF WORDS have been written — and even more preached — about the plagues of Egypt. This particular passage summarises a good many of them, but it is really worth reading the whole story, from chapter 7 to the end of chapter 12.

It goes something like this.

Moses and Aaron are instructed to ask royal permission for their people to leave the land in peace. They are promised magical — or perhaps hypnotic — powers, in order to convince Pharaoh of their divine authority. When this fails, they are to warn Pharaoh that the River Nile, the lifeblood and divinity of Egypt, will in some way be corrupted. This too will fail to convince Pharaoh, and in turn the following disasters will strike his land. Frogs — lice — flies — diseases of domestic animals — boils — hail — locusts — black darkness — death of the children.

Now these plagues represent a mounting crescendo of disaster. The water was a maddening inconvenience — but we are told that by digging sand-wells it could be filtered. The frogs smelled as they died, the lice itched, the flies tormented. But loss of herds was worse. Then came human suffering, loss of fruiting crops. For the locusts destroyed everything, blade as well as ear. Darkness breaks this increasing weight of horror, but only as a kind of "trailer" of the worse darkness to come, the darkness of death. The magicians recognised this sense of crescendo. For a time they could compete, but after the lice they threw in their hand — or their magic wand — at the same time. Though the rising tide of disaster seemed to insist on supernatural activity, each individual wave in it could be explained from natural causes. As telling little phrases imply, these were all situations which did in fact occur from time to time (e.g. verse 21 of chapter 9 draws a pleasing distinction between good employers and bad!). There

40

is in verse 32 of the same chapter an agricultural reference which seems to point the time of year: and verse 19 of chapter 10 stresses a "natural" explanation for the ending of the plague. In the same way, it has been suggested that the "blood" on the Nile was vegetable or bacterial in origin, like that "Red Death" which attacks fishing areas along the South African coast. This does not, of course, affect the point of the story. The God of nature is active in and through nature, rather than apart from it.

The question which really challenges us, of course, is summarised in chapter 9, verse 12 — "The Lord hardened the heart of Pharaoh". Are we indeed to suppose that God turned on the heat — and then conditioned Pharaoh psychologically so that it should remain switched on until the final furnace blast? Why not, in fact, just march the people out in the first instance, surrounded by a convenient cloud of magical darkness?

If we boil the carcass down to the bare bones, what *is* the essential skeleton of this story? Just this. The Hebrew people asked permission to leave the land in which they were serfs, and to emigrate in search of an independent homeland. They were refused it. Then followed a series of disasters, each normal in itself, but cumulative in result. Finally, Pharaoh associated these disasters with his refusal to the Hebrews and let them go. At the last moment, he changed his mind and sent troops in pursuit. They were overwhelmed whilst making a forced journey across sea-flats.

What strikes the reader here is the apparent and extraordinary obstinacy of Pharaoh, *if* indeed the connexion between the plagues and the continued presence of the Hebrews was really obvious. This obstinacy the Bible — which cannot accept, as we accept, the full extent of human free-will — must therefore put down to the divine account. It was unthinkable to the writers of the story that a man could have defied God — so they must suppose it is God himself who stiffens a man's pride to resist God. But no one can possibly tell — least of all an alien historian — what went on in the mind of the Egyptian monarch. Perhaps, indeed, this is the stubbornness of a furious despot, who stands out against the mounting pressure of public opinion until at last his own family is affected. Perhaps too, the connexion between the natural calamities and the Hebrew demand was not so clearly perceived. But what does certainly emerge from it all is the appalling power that tyranny and dictatorship possess — power to involve other and "innocent" people in disaster, simply because of their own obstinate refusal to recognise truth. When this happens in terms of contemporary history, we are apt to ask, "Why does God allow it?" The Old Testament writers found their explanation in the thought of a God whose activity was total and whose involvement was so complete that even dictators must be controlled, like puppets, by his hand. We find it more convincing to admit that, if freedom is granted to one, it must equally be available for others; that God does not cheat by altering his mind when things do not go exactly as he — or we — would wish; that if men will not learn their necessary relationship in one way, they must learn it by a worse.

EXODUS 12. 1–12

16

PASSOVER CELEBRATIONS

EVERY NATION HAS SOME MOMENT of history to which it looks back as its finest hour, the moment when it most fully shared all those qualities on whose possession it prides itself. Usually that moment has been one of deliverance.

It may be a deliverance from foreign invasion, from Persia at Marathon or from a Spanish Armada in the Channel. It may be of deliverance from starvation, as in Salt Lake City (where a monument commemorates the seagulls who devoured a plague of locusts), or from tyranny within, as France each July 14th rejoices to recall the storming of the Bastille. But it is always a moment when threatened or actual evil was somehow and wonderfully averted.

To the Jews, their escape from Egypt was the sum and total of all such moments. Formerly slaves, then they became free. Threatened by pursuing armies, they saw them wiped out. Faced

42

by appalling natural hazards, they saw the way miraculously opened. In that moment the God who had been nominally and potentially the God of Israel truly took them for his own, and proved to the whole earth the power of his protection. Psalm after psalm, legend after legend recalled it : the greatest of all their festivals, the Passover, was an annual reminder. It was a reminder they were to need in centuries to come, persecuted, ghetto-herded, coerced and tormented into apostasy from a faith they were over and over again denied the right to exercise.

Each returning spring saw them gathered round the family table, eating the unleavened bread, the bitter herbs and the Passover Lamb, and praying that next year they might keep the feast in Jerusalem. It has been suggested that this was originally a shepherd-feast, a thanksgiving for the fertility of the flock, the tribute of a nomad-people to the God who guided them on their endless march. But to the post-Egyptian Israel it was an act of gratitude for their past and of trust for the future — the reminder of God's covenant with them and of his power to deliver. It has too, even to this day, a sense of hospitality and shared happiness. Christianity has inherited from its ancestral Judaism a varying date for Easter (fixed, as was the Passover, by the lunar month of Nisan). It has also inherited the symbol of the Paschal Lamb sacrificed for others — and has transferred to Christmas something of Passover's hospitality and family happiness.

In accordance with that traditional hospitality, no family sits down to the Passover feast without opening the door to invite any hungry passer-by to share it : every table is laid with a wine-cup for the prophet who may come in to drink it.

Perhaps, in this day and age, we have become so apprehensive of the future that we have lost that sense of trust which Passover emphasises — we do not think enough of the occasions in our past, national or international, when man has been delivered from destruction. Six hundred years ago the Black Death killed off a third of our population, and men believed the end of the world was come. The fires in Chicago and in London, the earth-quakes of Messina and San Francisco, the invasions of Moor and Tartar, all these seemed to men to be indeed the end of their world. But after each, life began again, through each of them life was strangely and wonderfully preserved.

Whatever the cruelty and stupidity of man, we may surely trust that God will not allow him totally and absolutely to destroy the human race. There is a strange and fascinating book (long out of print) by M. P. Shiel, called *The Purple Cloud*. It tells of a world completely wiped out by a strange cosmic poisonous gas. Or rather — NOT completely. One man survives (he was on the polar cap at the time). And he finds one woman, a child who had been trapped in the Turkish catacombs. At first he defies their common salvation, proud that he is free to refuse a share in creating a new humanity, able, if he wishes, to be the last man of all. But the book ends with his acceptance of destiny, with a new Adam and Eve sailing away together to start the human race all over again.

Behind this fable lies some comfort for us in our perilous age, the belief that God still has faith in man, however often that faith may be betrayed. As we look back on the last decade, and consider how often and how close we have been to total war, that comfort may well be strengthened. "Not unto us, O Lord, not unto us, but to thy name be the praise."

Exodus 14. 19–31

17

SALVATION BY WATER

To Israel, AS WE HAVE SAID, the crossing of the Red Sea was its moment of destiny. They came to the shore as a huddle of poorly armed fugitives, loaded with possessions, driving before them a great herd of farm stock. (Presumably many of these were slaughtered for food at an early date, before grazing became too much of a problem.)

And then, surrounded by the desert, with only water before them, they saw dust clouds in the distance and realised that mobile armed columns were plunging down upon them. But what happened? First, their pursuers failed to make contact with them. Perhaps the great gale from the east that rose up blew the sand into their faces, whilst the Israelites, with only water before them, were unaffected. At all events, the attack was not pressed home — and the fugitives found that they could make their way in safety through the shallows or over the mudflats. And when the Egyptians followed, the narrow wheels of their chariots bogged down in the soft going, and the water, returning, over-whelmed them. It is quite impossible, at this length of time, to explain with any certainty what happened. All that we know is that this incident impressed itself forever on the Jewish mind and was carried over into the new Israel of the church. Delight-ing, as the early Christians did, to find prototypes or anticipa-tions of the New Testament in the Old, they spoke of the water of baptism as the Red Sea, through which the Christians must pass to begin his new life. To us the parallel may seem far-fetched and awkward — but it may have a closer application than we suppose. For, to the Jews, this was the Moment of Truth, the point from which there could be no turning back. They emerged from the waters as a *nation*, forming its own high and demanding destiny.

In the same way, many of us can look back to a point of decision in our own lives. It may have been the choice of a faith — a job — a husband or wife. But it was a true moment of decision and from it there could and can be no turning back. Now the Israelites were often, after the Red Sea crossing, to be afraid, often to be forgetful of their calling, often to regret the comforts they had left behind. But to have tried to go back would have been to die as a nation, to refuse their vocation. It is the same with us. Hard as life often is, much as we may wish it could have been different, we too must be committed to it. There is no going back upon that choice we made — and, indeed, if we could reverse it, those Egyptian fleshpots might still be a mirage and we should find instead the taskmaster's whip and the bricks that must be made without straw. Curiously another watery crossing has given us a synonym for this moment of decision. Julius Caesar, the appointed general of the Roman people, hastened back victorious from the wars and reached the frontier of Italy. That frontier was marked by a little river, the "Rubicon" — either he must disband his army, and return

as a private citizen to a nation tormented with civil disturbance
— or else he would keep his army in being and thereby outlaw
himself by claiming the power of a dictator. Caesar chose. He
"crossed the Rubicon".

Exodus 16. 11–26

18

BREAD FROM HEAVEN

THE GREAT JOURNEY OF ISRAEL
through the desert included many events which they regarded
as "miraculous", as evidence, that is, of God's special concern for
them. The *means* of miracle may have been events that occur in
the ordinary course of nature — but the fact that they occurred
when they did, at a time of special need, assured the recipients
of their significance. Thus, flocks of quail are often driven by
the wind, but there was one occasion when such a weary flock
landed just at the moment of Israel's need.

Most of these events were unique, special individual occasions,
but there were at least two of what can be called "continuous
miracles", or extraordinary happenings which went on regularly
over an extended period. These are, first, the "pillar of cloud
and/or fire" which guided the people and, second, the manna
that sustained them.

What was the factual nature of these events? Some people
prefer to think of them as something utterly outside the course of
nature; others would see in them the appreciation by men of the
possibilities within nature, and of the way in which these can
be intelligently used.

In the latter interpretation, the "pillar of cloud by day and fire
by night" may perfectly well be a volcano, seen far away across
the desert, a landmark towards which a column on the march
could direct its course. If, at a critical moment, the people were
led out of desperate danger by such a far-seen beacon, then it
would become printed on their national memory. And as for

manna? Most of the natural explanations offered seem rather unconvincing. An edible gum distilled from a plant, even a fungus or mushroom discovered to provide a possible foodstuff — these do not really seem to match the story or explain the impression of divine intervention.

Perhaps therefore all we can say with certainty is that the Israelites *did* discover in the desert some form of foodstuff which was outside their previous experience, but which was capable of supporting life.

From these two experiences, they made two deductions, which have had immense influence on religious thinking ever since.

The first was the idea of *"guidance"*. This, however expressed, means the conviction that man can discover the will of God for him in each situation of daily life, and that, in following out that will, he fulfils his individual purpose and finds his fullest satisfaction. The difficulty here is that of discovering what is genuinely the will of God and what is only the prompting of the individual's subconscious. The latter, when apparently endorsed by divine authority, produces that devastating self-righteousness which has led to wars and persecutions innumerable, and is in itself one of the most disagreeable of all qualities. "Guidance" needs, therefore, to be most carefully checked against the whole pattern of faith, the more so when it conflicts with the ordinary rules of charity and tolerance. Still, in the last extreme, even the most authoritative of churches recognises its supremacy. A time may come when a man or woman says, "God leads me in this direction" — and then he or she *must* follow, or be found faithless.

The second association for us is that of manna and the "daily bread" for which we pray.

Now all our normal instincts are in favour of security. Brought up on the story of the cautious ant, we regard it as our moral duty to prepare for the future, and to be ready for that "rainy day" which is — in our climate and economy — quite sure to come.

Yet the Christian is most urgently commanded *not* to think about tomorrow, to be content with the moment, to expect only his present maintenance. Does this really mean that it is wrong to save and wicked to stock our larder? or that a bank book is a passport to hell, and an insurance policy evidence of lack of faith? Is it a condemnation of all forward planning, and an encouragement to "flirt the time gloriously"? Surely not. Again and again the Bible speaks of plan and purpose, of acceptance of destiny, of the need to travel as with certainty to an intended goal.

Perhaps we need to combine the meanings of the pillar and the bread, and to see a significance in their relationship. Called, then, to go out into the unknown, we go in the belief that, when all the techniques of experience fail us, new resources will be revealed. We *are* to use our own powers, we *are* to husband them carefully and spend them with sense — but when they are so spent, new ones will be made available.

Yet the bread that is provided, the help that is given, is for a purpose, and must be used accordingly. We may be generous in God's service, but not extravagant in our own. Those who rely on divine support must be quite sure they deserve it. Wasteful inefficiency is not to be explained away as Christian trust, nor failure to anticipate events identified with faith. Somehow we have to keep a balance — and how difficult this can be! Should a church or charitable organisation, for instance, have a cash reserve in the bank, or should it spend as it receives? There is never an easy answer, and the prudent will always be suspicious of the spenders, the spenders critical of the prudent. Perhaps the only safe rule for each of us is to detect our own inclination and then try to balance it by moving in the other direction!

EXODUS 20. 1–17

19

THE TEN COMMANDMENTS

THERE IS A DIFFERENCE BETWEEN our idea of what is legal and our idea of what is right, though the two may often overlap. For instance, we do not arrest people for lying (fortunately for many people engaged in the business of newspaper production, in politics, and in advertising), yet we do punish them if convicted of perjury, libel or forgery, areas of conduct in which lying demonstrably affects our authority, well-being, or property.

There is continual argument as to where and how far overlap should occur. "You cannot make people good by Act of Parliament." Perhaps, but you can make it much easier, by punishing them if they are bad. The area over which legal and moral responsibility coincide is continually extending and includes today children and employees. Customers and employers are still marginal!

A perfect legal code would, presumably, be one in which the laws were good, just, and of such nature as good men would find pleasure in keeping. But this code would need to be accompanied by a universal religion which enabled everybody to think of goodness and justice in the same terms.

This is what the Ten Commandments tried very hard to do — to identify personal goodness with social justice and to harness the energy of personal morality, so as to strengthen the rule of law. They include social directions no less than personal exhortation.

From this point of view, the Third Commandment is an insistence on the integrity of the solemn oath — in itself the foundation of all commercial and political trust. Yet is there today any promise, however solemn, which the nation is prepared to uphold?

The Fourth Commandment insists that everybody, including the domestic animals, should have a regular day off; the Fifth is the ancestor of old-age pensions and social welfare.

The scope of the Sixth Commandment includes legislation, for example, as to road-safety and inflammable toys.

The Seventh needs little comment today, whilst the Eighth opens up to scrutiny the world of commercial reality. The Ninth queries our accepted use of the "smear" in commercial and political dispute, whilst the Tenth attacks our acquisitive society from the root up. Nine and Ten together certainly call a halt to much commercial publicity.

At the same time, the Ten Commandments are a personal

code. They recognise that individual interpretation of law is the essential part of its full observation, and that the man of divided mind and loyalty is incapable of accurate interpretation. So they begin by emphasising the continuing traditions of moral purpose and personal devotion which must unite the nation within itself and link it with its historical past. To unite, there must be unity. So the whole nation must share one faith and one loyalty. The God who is the focus of this loyalty must be more than man-sized. This is why he is not to be identified with any possible object, or limited to any one representation. For, to represent an object or a person is in some sense to limit them to that representation and to eliminate possible alternatives. Yet God must, of his very nature, be greater than any one possible representation, if he is to include all representation. Christ is Son of Man — and men are black and white — hook- or snub-nosed, fair-haired or dark. Somehow, man's local and specialised loyalty to tradition and community and state must be included within the wider loyalty to mankind and divinity, his neighbour and his god. The Ten Commandments, perhaps beyond all other attempts, do continue to set before us a moral imperative which combines a code of social behaviour, suitable to all men everywhere, with an idea of paramount and universal duty.

EXODUS 32. 1–24

20

THE GOLDEN CALF

ONE OF THE PROBLEMS OF LIFE is the rapidity of its change. One moment we are on top of the world, feeling fine, money in the bank, the sun in the sky; next moment, a child has run into the street, a car has swerved, there's blood on the road and misery in the heart. We come out of church full of uplift and devotion — and in no time we've started a quarrel. This is true of individuals, and it is no less true — as every wise politician knows — of nations. The Bible is full of evidence of it — and possibly politicians were wiser men when they were also students of the Bible.

This story is a case in point. Moses has gone up to Mount Sinai to receive the Law — to listen to the voice of God, and to think out a constitution, initiate a legal system — or however you like to put it. The people, meantime, are to wait quietly. But waiting quietly is the hardest thing in the world to do. They decide that Moses is probably dead, and that it is now up to them to appoint his successor. And this time they will not make the mistake of having a "Leader", who will make stern demands in the name of an invisible and righteous God. They will have a "high priest", a technical expert to handle the organisation of religion, and they will have a God who is a symbol at the same time of fertility and of prosperity. They will have a comfortable man-size religion, which will simply endorse and sanctify their own attitude to life.

Moses erupts into the situation, and deals with it as any strong man does with a palace revolution. Nothing could be more revealing than the respective attitudes of Moses and Aaron at this point. Moses is a kind of Christ-figure, appealing for forgiveness for others, setting this immediate lapse against the whole pattern of Israel and the divine purpose — utterly refusing the glory offered him in verse 10, and identifying himself with the very people who have rejected him.

Aaron, on the other hand, blames it all on someone else — and even on an accident. The excuse he offers in verses 22 to 24 is about as shoddy as any excuse could be. He is of those who rule by Gallup poll: that which people want, he is prepared to give them. It is never his fault — even though one of the results of his policy is that the camp is without arms or defence against possible attack.

So the chapter ends — a chapter rich in matter for thought — with punishment and rededication, with Moses once again accepting his share of blame for what has happened, since these are *his* people and *his* responsibility.

The whole story illustrates the tension in which the church must continually exist. It has got to be in the World, but its head must be in the clouds. All the pressure is on it to provide people with what they want — which is justification for the agreeable materialism which so easily enshrouds us. Technical progress and material prosperity have brought us out of the Egypt of the past. So let us worship their techniques and offer to them our resources.

Let us, we say, have a church which is "efficient" and "well-organised". Let us study the techniques of salesmanship and communication. Let us hallow our contemporary pattern of life, and let us turn our backs on the disquieting voices of the prophets.

And let us hope that we do not become thereby naked to our own worst enemy. For it is the responsibility of the church to be the salt of life, at once its savour and its preservative. Yet the salt is not the same as the food which it seasons — and if it becomes merely a part of that food, it ceases to fulfil its purpose. Food becomes tasteless and unsatisfactory *without* salt — yet salt is impossible as food on its own account. The world and the church need each other, and each only finds true fulfilment in a right relationship to the other.

EXODUS 35. 20–29

21

TENT MEETING

IT IS DOUBTFUL IF ANY NORMAL Bible-reader ever manages to read right through the chapters describing "the tabernacle". What with badger-skins and pomegranates, "taches" (whatever these may be) and chapiters, mitres and breeches — there seems very little connexion with anything related either to our experience or to our comprehension.

But the *idea* of the tabernacle is worth study, however unimportant its details may be. For it is an *idea* that we need to rediscover in our church-planning.

Our churches, that is to say, are all of them based upon one or more of certain Biblical concepts — the Temple, the Synagogue, the High Place, or the Upper Room. By the *Temple* we mean the holy Establishment, the group of buildings, all devoted to some sort of religious function, and staffed by a group of professionals. Such, for instance, is the average cathedral.

The *Synagogue* is a place of assembly for teaching, the preaching-house, or conventicle. Methodist Central Halls and Anglican churches of the eighteenth century are cases in point.

The *High Place* is a shrine, a place where holiness dwells; it may be a little quiet chapel in the heart of a city, or a lonely ruin on a clifftop. Usually it has some traditional association of sanctity: sometimes there is an awe about it which is near to terror.

And the *Upper Room* is the place of Communion, where the family meet about their common table. It may be big as Chartres, small as Stoke Charity; no matter, the purpose is the same.

But all of them are *places,* fixed and stable places. Now the whole point of the tabernacle is that it moves about. It is, as you might say, quite literally "with it". The people who have a tabernacle do not need a God-enfolding holy city. The tabernacle is just one of their own travelling houses: it goes where they go — and when it goes, God goes too. He is always there, right on their own tent-lintel.

Inside the tabernacle is the *"Ark"* — which means "chest". It seems to have been a big wooden case, resembling in shape a seat or throne. Inside it were placed from time to time objects embodying the history of the people, so that it became a kind of incarnation of their past. (Maybe Lenin's body in Red Square and Westminster Abbey in London have a little of the same significance.) The Ark was itself the focus or distillation of the holiness of the tabernacle, a totem object so powerful that it was dangerous to knock it over even by accident.

Now there is about this idea of a moving sanctuary something worth our thought. If the purpose of acts of worship is that man and God should meet, is it necessary that they always meet in the same place? The tabernacle moved around where people were : it didn't stay put and expect them to come to it. Is not most of our own ecclesiastical thinking based on the latter concept?

Why, when a new housing area needs a church, should we not experiment with a caravan — or tabernacle church — a building that could open up on the site as soon as the first householders moved in — and then itself move on? Why do we *have* to build a "temple-church" in every single area? Why indeed can we not experiment with that version of the tabernacle — the "house-church", the use of people's own homes as the scene of worship?

Far away and long ago it may be — but at least the tabernacle gave to the wandering tribes the sure sense of a God who was involved in their problems, shared in their privations, rejoiced in their victories. He belonged to them — and they belonged to him. It was this same thought that Christ renewed and enriched in the service of Holy Communion. God, he taught his friends, is to be found everywhere about us, active in the every day. He does not need the remote splendour of a temple, if we can offer him the hospitality of an upper room.

EXODUS 35. 30–36

22

CRAFT UNION

WE HAVE A REGRETTABLE TENdency to suppose there is something called "religious art" (as distinct from any other sort of art) — so that we have religious art suppliers, religious wine growers, religious drama producers. And these provide us with a curious specialised range of products, easily recognisable but hard to specify.

It is these products which we tend to associate with church life, irrespective of their quality. Which means, without regard to the effect produced by their quality or lack of it. Yet if we believe indeed in a creator God who has given us our share in

54

the responsibility of continuing creation, if we believe that we are called to build "the Kingdom of God" — by which, presumably, we mean a world obedient to God and ordered as he would have it — then we shall be concerned continually with this matter of quality. We shall say, "Is this drama *good,* by the standards of goodness proper to drama?" not "Is this play about a parson, and does it deduce an appropriate moral?" We shall see that the quality of "goodness" in cooking is not the same as that of piety in the cook (though one hopes that one might produce the other). And we shall recognise quality in craftsmanship as something which comes from God and pays its own tribute to him. We talk sentimentally — but perhaps also rightly — of flowers and birds as praising God by their very existence: we need also to think of "artefacts" — objects made by man — as praising the God by whom they are originally inspired. This is the whole tenor of this present passage. Here are two men who have been "called by name" by God: two men who have been given a literal "vocation". They are chosen out as artists and craftsmen: like all such men whose greatness is real, they want to share their skill with others and to teach them. So they become foremen or supervisors, enlisting and training others of similar ability. But the picture is not only of concerned and committed experts. All sorts of ordinary people come in on it, providing whatever they can of raw or partly finished materials.

This is a delightful picture of the supremacy of ability — and, in turn, of the "social responsibility" which ought to be part of such ability. These are not artists working in a vacuum, unappreciated by the crowd whom they themselves despise. These are recognised masters, whom other men are proud to assist in any way they can. The masters, in turn, work for the community. And *all* of them, masters, journeymen, unskilled labour, are filled with pride and joy in the exercise of their own special gift. For this gift, it is recognised, comes from God, and is a trust from him. For them *not* to use it — or to use it unworthily — would therefore be to deny God's will, to sin against the light. If this seems very different from our own attitude to expertise, in art or science or industry — which attitude is in fact the more sensible? How good it is to see the greatest of men humbled as they realise how far short the effort must fall of the dream, how needful it is to pass on to other people knowledge and experience which they in their turn may use better than we have done.

23

CLEAN AND UNCLEAN

WHEN WE ARE CONFRONTED WITH practices that seem totally foreign to all our patterns of thought, it is as well to begin with an attempt to understand their original purpose. *Why* did people behave like this? What was the situation or problem with which they had to deal? Only when this is clear can we assess the efficacy or otherwise of the technique.

Now much of the book of Leviticus is taken up with interminable accounts of "uncleanness", and how to put it right. This "uncleanness" is a feature both of Judaism and of Hinduism; it is expressed in three ways. First, there is the unclean contact. The mere touching of that which is officially unclean produces a contagion which must somehow be removed. Second, there is unclean consumption, food or drink which for one reason or another is forbidden. Third, there is unclean behaviour, the action which of its nature defiles a man. If this is deliberate, it is sin: if accidental, it must be purified and remedied.

The basic idea behind uncleanness is that behind all practice of taboo. "Taboo" is a mark of separation. It may be separation between groups, the religious activities in which only initiated males may share, the secret rites of women, the wearing of a caste mark or special clothing. Or it may mark off an entire group — as the Sikhs, for instance, are marked off by the five symbols of their faith.

There need not be any logical reason for a particular expression of difference or for a mark of separation. It is quite enough that the separated groups *are* different. (Probably the nearest parallel in our own society is the privilege system of

English boarding schools. Here special language, special oddities of dress, special areas of the building or even special physical postures are restricted to members of an appropriate group. Uncleanness, then, is incurred by the deliberate or accidental breaking of the barriers of separation. It is the negative aspect of that ritual purity and racial dedication which was the pride of Judaism. Where there is this sense of "apartness" (call it "holiness" if you will), there must also be a sense of "uncleanness" when that "apartness" is in any way infringed.

This purity or "apartness", therefore, must always be hedged about and delimited with walls which it was "defilement" to cross, even accidentally. However, since accidents will happen, elaborate rituals were constructed for those who did accidentally err. (Note that the failure *must* be accidental, and not deliberate. This is a mechanism for cleansing a stain, not forgiving a sin.)

Now, to some extent, such rules of defilement are sensible sanitary precautions, or at least sensible attempts to discover what sanitary precautions are effective. (We see something like them every time there is a small-pox scare.) A healthy people encountering infectious disease is perfectly right to suspect and destroy all possible forms of contagion, even if — as in the second passage above — this may only have been fungus. But we, who suffer from dry rot and death-watch beetle (not to mention bed bugs) can scarcely sneer at sensible destruction. The trouble is that sensible destruction can develop into merciless killing, when the plague-spot happens to be human. Self-preservation, whether it be of body or soul, is not always the law of life, since it means death to others.

Our own society, of course, offers some curious parallels. In its anxiety to maintain its integrity, it can resort to racial laws and restrictions, to suspicion of the foreigner and his influence. To maintain its freedom, it "purges" (the very word is significant) the Communist and the Fascist.

Within itself, it produces class-distinctions of speech and manner. It has certain vocabularies proper to the groups it contains. Some years ago, even styles in clothing were different (a particularly virulent plum-purple was considered in

Britain the proper colour of leisure-wear suiting for lower-paid workers); today, clothing distinction is a mark of personal disposition and appropriate age-group, rather than social class.

We may, that is to say, no longer use categories of "clean" and "unclean", substituting instead "superior" and "common". We may blur the distinctions and make "purification" easier: but we still dig our ditches and erect our walls. We still find satisfaction in identifying ourselves with a group and thereby excluding ourselves from other such. Only notice the costumes adopted by supporters of rival football teams!

Nor are the members of a segregated group themselves averse to the formation of splinter groups-within-groups. The moment adolescents as an age-class have discovered a common uniform is the very moment in which they begin to discover new and significant differences amongst themselves. Each despised immigrant group waits for the next group to arrive that they may have the pleasure themselves of despising in turn.

LEVITICUS 25. 1–17

24

SOIL CONSERVATION

"Hurrah, hurrah, we sing the Jubilee
Hurrah, hurrah, the song that makes you free."

EVERYONE KNOWS WHAT WE mean by a "jubilee". The word itself is the Latin one to be found in the name of the canticle *Jubilate*. It just means "rejoicing". We think of a jubilee as a time of celebration as we look back on years of life, whether of a church or a royal person or an institution.

But in the beginning it was a social experiment of considerable importance—not to mention its agricultural significance. For one of the important points of the Jewish code was its recognition of the value of the "holy-day" or rest period. This was

58

granted, as their divine right, to the beast, the stranger, and the slave, as well as to the freeborn.

But a single day's respite from ploughing is not much use to the soil, so the principle was carried further. As living creatures took their holiday one day in seven, so the land should get *its* turn, one year in seven. This leaving the soil to lie fallow is a real attempt towards soil conservation : it is, too, a recognition that the good earth has its rights, and that these rights are to be respected. When man fails in this respect, trouble follows — as the dust-bowls of the earth remind us.

But when they are properly regarded, then the soil continues to yield and to yield more and more. The soil, for instance, of farming Europe, is — or was — capable of a far higher yield than that of India, simply because it had been properly fed and properly rested. Long ago, the Jews saw this perfectly clearly and wrote the need and duty of it into their code of law. A pity, perhaps, that we who think of land chiefly as a source of capital gain for building and development should have lost that sense of responsibility.

But they went further. Seven was the holy number, seven times seven the very perfection of number. When this was reached there came a year seven times more important than the sabbatical year — the year of freedom, or jubilee. It was called the year of freedom, because it was the year in which debts were cancelled, pledged goods returned, and slaves made free. No debtor, this meant, was ever to be without hope, like the Indian peasant in the grip of the money-lender. There was always the year of jubilee to which to look forward. This is why the Armies of the north, marching through Georgia, sang of jubilee as the "song that makes you free". They came in arms to set the slave free, as, so long before, the law of God had set the debtor free.

The principle of jubilee, then, was a simple one. No system of economics, no necessity of intensive cultivation, was to be allowed to dominate the moral Law. Man and soil both had a right to freedom — and this right was not only written, as it were, into the nation's constitution but guaranteed by a safe-guard. It is a sad comment on human weakness that there is grave uncertainty as to whether this year of jubilee was ever, in fact, enforced!

25

CALEB AND JOSHUA

MANY OF US, AS CHILDREN, were baffled by the extraordinary slowness of Israel as they migrated between Egypt and Canaan. Even our infant legs would have covered the distance in a fraction of the forty years they are supposed to have taken. Why, Livingstone crossed and re-crossed Africa, Paul covered most of the known world, in less time than they appear to have taken on one of their stages.

But this is, of course, to misunderstand the nature of their nomadic life. These are not a people marching steadily towards a final goal, but a desert tribe circling from oasis to oasis, making tentative experiments at settlement, welcomed by a few, stoutly resisted by others. It is a long-term game of "musical chairs". And, marching, fighting, breeding, squabbling, they are being forged into a nation. A rabble of runaway slaves left Egypt: an organised and disciplined army at last entered Canaan. All this took time — a full lifetime, says the story.

Now the conquest of Canaan was certainly not as total as Jewish history liked to believe. Contemporary evidence suggests much more of an infiltration, with pockets of the original inhabitants holding out for many years to come. After all, it was extremely difficult for people without anything remotely corresponding to artillery to capture walled cities. When this *was* done, it was frequently done by craft rather than force. In addition, many of the local inhabitants were very tough characters indeed, who had survived plenty of previous invasions, and were on their guard against any new one. Amongst them were the "children of Anak", men of tremendous stature (perhaps resembling in this the lion-hunting Masai of today) who had not unnaturally chosen to live in the fertile and well-watered southern end of Palestine, amongst a variety of scarcely less militant neighbours. This is tribal territory, divided amongst clans as in mediaeval Scotland or contemporary East Africa.

Now the bravest of the Hebrews were all for fighting it out on the spot. They brought visual evidence of the soil-yield, and they urged a head-on attack. Not so the more timid — and, one must feel, some sympathy for them. The fighting men were encumbered with women, children and domestic animals; they had no base of operations and no large-scale military training. Better, was their prudent advice, to elect a new leader and make for the safety of Egypt.

But, though their advice seemed reasonable, it was, in fact, bad. There are moments when the only right decision is to go in the face of all reason: the French, at Verdun, deciding that as both wings were in danger, and the centre unstable, the army would now attack: Christopher Columbus, reaching the stage when half the ship's provisions were exhausted and the only security lay in return — and then going on. All history is full of such precedents, even though it is sometimes discreet as to the gamble that *didn't* come off.

The real difference between the Calebs and Joshuas of this world and the cautious scouts is simply that of belief. If we really do believe that we are doing God's will, then no odds in the world should frighten us — and Athanasius can stand alone. This is why the great victories have been won, and the greatest activities built up, by single individuals or small groups who *knew*, beyond argument, what they had to do. Then they proceeded to do it. But we need to be quite sure that it *is* God's will we set out to do, rather than the rash impulse of our own subconscious, or a desperate throw to justify our own lack of prevision. We cannot suppose God is much concerned with enabling us to defy the laws of logistics or the reasonable standards of expectation — indeed the New Testament flatly asserts the contrary (Luke 14, verses 31 to 33). Perhaps, then, it is wrong to say the difference is one of "belief", since belief may be wrongheaded and unjustified. The belief must itself be true. And how can we know that it is? That is, so often, the nub and core of our problem. Is it better to give unquestioning assent — with all the dynamic that may follow — or to allow humility and charity to lessen our conviction and, perhaps, cloud the springs of action?

26

BALAAM'S ASS

THIS IS EXACTLY THE SORT OF story that makes the critic of the Bible laugh. Here is something in the tradition of Brer Rabbit or Red Riding Hood, a fairy story of militant angels and talking animals. What can it possibly mean for our day and age, what possible truth of fact can it represent? Then take it, for the moment, just as a story.

Balak, King of the border-people of Moab (they lived on the east of Jordan, and for much of Hebrew history played the part of Red Indians to western settlers) is extremely anxious as he watches the immigrant caravans winding their way across his upland territories. So he decides to invoke supernatural help, and sends to a celebrated holy-man or wizard, named, rather confusingly, Balaam. He asks for a comforting oracle, and offers a good price for it.

Balaam proceeds to consult divine authority. And here we come across a fascinating implication. Balaam *cannot* have been a Jew, in the full sense, since he is there in the country when the Jews arrive. What is the God he worships? How is he to be equated with the God of Israel? The text suggests that as a man of faith, trying to get in touch with God, he does make effective contact. This idea, that there is but one God and that all who genuinely try to pray do indeed pray to the same God, was to disappear from religious history and is even now barely accepted. But our story insists that this shaman medicine-man of long ago heard the voice of that God whom men were to know face to face in Jesus Christ. And he knew very clearly that he *could* not pronounce the kind of oracle the King wanted.

But, like most of us, he is anxious to compromise. Unlike most of us, though, he is not for sale, even for a "house full of silver and gold". (The strange verse 20 must represent his effort to maintain his technical integrity, whilst doing his utmost to oblige the king: it is his own rationalisation of the situation, and not the voice of conscience.)

So he saddles his donkey and off he goes. But it is not to be an uninterrupted journey. All, perhaps, one needs to say about the incident that follows is that it reminds us that animals, too, are God's creatures and may be much more percipient of invisible truth than we are. Everyone knows stories, for instance, of dogs and horses which dislike certain places as frightening — even if we are much too optimistic about their gift of discrimination about human beings!

Because of this, God, who cares about the fallen sparrow, can communicate in his own way through the animal world, and so Balaam has to learn at the lips of his old friend and companion, the ass. Not only that, but she saves Balaam's life into the bargain.

The rest of the story is long, but well worth reading. This is a tale of a king, almost inexhaustibly patient in his anxiety to get the oracle he wants, and of a prophet's quite inexhaustible determination not to let him have it. It includes some magnificent passages of poetry (specially chapter 24, verses 15 to 17) — and it ends with an impressive act of tolerance by Balak — who, in spite of his not unnatural indignation, lets Balaam go in peace — or perhaps the life of a holy man was regarded as more sacrosanct to a Moabite heathen than it was to a Jewish king — or than it has since been to Christian authorities.

Have we, who limit our channels of religious communication not only to the appropriate faith but usually to our accepted denomination within it, really a more splendid and embracing vision of an omnipotent God than these "fairy-story writers" of long ago, to whom every genuine "seer" really saw truth, and to whom the humble animals were holy?

DEUTERONOMY 4. 41–43; JOSHUA 20

27

ESCAPISTS ALL

THE BLOOD FEUD OR "VENDETTA" is or has been part of the social structure of many nations, from Arabia to Afghanistan and from Corsica to Kentucky. The system is simple. If a member of one family is killed by a member of another, then it is incumbent upon *any* member of the aggrieved group to kill *any* member of the assaulting one. The process continues indefinitely — indeed, until all recollection of the original incident is lost. For a vivid account of the working of such feuds, it would be hard to beat Mark Twain's description in *Huckleberry Finn.*

Now there is a kind of primitive pseudo-justice about the vendetta, a sense of tribal solidarity — but this very reliance on solidarity removes it from the spheres of equity and reason. Like the duel, it takes justice away from the community, who can consider the case dispassionately, and makes the injured group its own avenger.

The alternative offered by Mosaic Law was a good one. The aggrieved party — whether person or family — was entitled to a fair compensation, or a fair revenge — "an eye for an eye and a tooth for a tooth". They could take it in cash or take it out in kind. But how to make sure they got only the due pound of flesh? How to make sure that justice was administered by those not emotionally involved?

Today we manage this by the use of police and a judiciary. The injured person is not allowed to exact a penalty: he dials 999 and the matter is taken out of his hands. Indeed, many of us think that it has gone too far out of his hands and that some element of compensation to the injured should be added to that of penalty for the offence.

But in a society where there are no police, what is to prevent the wronged person dealing out justice in his own fashion? Only the attitude that the law will hold him responsible. And if the offence is very great, the provocation immense, that restraint may be inadequate.

Here comes in the idea of the "city of refuge", or the "sanctuary" which was claimed within the Church in mediaeval times. The city of refuge was a device to enable the unwitting murderer, the man who by anger or carelessness or sheer mischance had caused another's death, to submit his cause to an impartial tribunal. If he could escape hot-foot to a city of refuge, and could convince its leading citizens that this was manslaughter and not murder, he could live there in sanctuary until his case was debated before the general assembly of the people. The whole nation thus took over from the family responsibility for seeing that justice was truly done.

Now we have still our cities of refuge, though we give them many names. Most of us need a bolt-hole of escape from a world where we seem to be misunderstood, to be blamed for wrongs we never did, to be suspected of motives we never made ours: we join clubs and societies, grow dahlias, catch fish; or we plan ocean voyages in small sailing boats, study the stars, dress up as Red Indians, attend seances. We get away from it all, and forget the avenger of blood, the mutter of the world's traffic, and the trial which must one day be faced.

Such "escapes" do us no harm if they are only temporary cities of refuge, places where we may draw our breath, order our minds and steady our nerves before we go back to meet the situation we left behind. But no one should live for ever in a city of refuge, unless he has turned his back on humanity — an abdication from his share of human responsibility. The whole point of a city of refuge was that its gates stood open to welcome the panting runner, not shut to defend the latest refugee from reality. While we live, there can be no escape from life. And to force one by suicide has always been considered the act of a coward.

DEUTERONOMY 20

28

HOW TO ORGANISE AN ARMY

THERE ARE, TRADITIONALLY, TWO ways in which to build up a military striking force. The first is in terms of power. This used to mean "manpower". Provide enough in sheer weight of numbers, and, like an ant army on the march, you will go forward whilst gradually beating down all opposition, however fearful your own losses. But today

E

it means "weapon-power". The appalling text on the machine-gun memorial in London announces with satisfaction that "Saul hath slain his thousands: David his tens of thousands". Any future memorial to the designers or firers of intercontinental ballistic missiles could substitute millions for tens of thousands. To have a nuclear weapon is more significant than to have justice on your side.

But even "weapon-power" is not in itself sufficient. You need, secondly, skilled and determined hands to wield the weapons. This is why Cromwell wanted his Ironsides to know what they were fighting for, and to believe in it. This is behind Sir John Moore's creation of light-infantry, independent, responsible, mobile troops with a pride in themselves and their unit. This is behind all ideas of "indoctrination", however degraded this may be from the original. And this is why intelligent generals have always asked for troops who should combine a degree of volunteer enthusiasm with professional techniques, as against obedient masses of conscripted cannon-fodder.

The Hebrews were very well aware of this. This very chapter begins with a kind of Montgomery pep-talk, with the priest playing the role of the commissar in Russian revolutionary forces and being responsible for morale. It goes on with military "welfare". Make sure that none of the troops have domestic problems or wife-trouble, that their heart is in the coming battle and not back home where there's difficulty. See to regular receipt of mail, and that pay-allotments have got through all right.

And then, what about the "battle-shock" case, or the man whose nerve has gone, or who never had one to go? Do you shoot deserters? Not a bit. Get rid of them. Send them home: advice so advanced that it has seldom, if ever, been taken in armies ever since it was given.

We go on to the rules of war. First, always offer terms, give people the chance to make peace. And when they reject it—fight until you win. Afterwards? Here comes the part out of which one would like to think we have grown. As regards neighbour territories spare the women and children, but wipe out the fighting men. Deprive them of any hope or possibility of rebellion. But as regards the places you propose to occupy, utterly and totally annihilate.

After this repellent passage, it comes as a little relief to find that the rules of war forbid you to destroy the trees (olive, vine, and the rest) upon which life depends, except in so far as you need them for siege-works. In other words, no "scorched-earth" policy. You've got to live there yourself some day and you're going to need those trees!

We are accustomed to criticise the Old Testament, comparing its standards unfavourably with the New. Yet, though we ought never to revert to its standards when they are — as they sometimes are — demonstrably below our own, we may with advantage learn from them when they are superior to ours. If power politics are still to be employed, then let us remember that they themselves stand under judgement and that Means are as much subject to criticism as Ends. After all, over and again it is the Means we use which subtly and secretly alter the intended Ends themselves.

DEUTERONOMY 22. 1–11

29

FINDINGS NOT KEEPINGS

THE BOOK OF DEUTERONOMY IS A fascinating hotch-potch, which ranges from the proper digging of latrines (chapter 23, verses 12 to 14) to principles of charity distribution (chapter 24, verses 19 to 21). It takes a stiff line with juvenile delinquents (chapter 21, verses 18 to 21), a generous one with accidental death (chapter 19, verses 4 to 6) and runaway servants (chapter 23, verses 15 and 16), and a sensible one with fortune-tellers (chapter 18, verse 22). But the common principles involved all the way through are simple, and are well illustrated in this particular passage. The first is that of *Goodwill*. Each person is expected to behave in a neighbourly way to every other one. This means not only a respect for the property-rights of another (chapter 19, verse 14), but a readiness to help him. Verse 4, for instance, is one we all need to recall before passing by a stranded motorist on a lonely road. The poor and the unfortunate have a rightful claim upon us.

The second is that of *Respect for the Natural World*. Man is entitled to get his livelihood from it, but not at the cost of destroying it. This is illustrated by verses 6 and 7 of this chapter : it is fair to take the eggs, but we should leave the mother bird to lay another clutch.

Verse 8 illustrates the third principle, that of *Reasonable Consideration*. We are to anticipate what may happen through our carelessness or another's, and to take action to avoid it. Such is the attitude of the sensible driver, who assumes that everyone else is both incompetent and dangerous — and so avoids the accident that would *not* have been his fault, as well as the one that would have been. The principle is also applied in assessing guilt in the complicated matrimonial situations which follow later.

The fourth principle is that which it is hardest for the modern mind to understand. It can be called the principle of *Integrity* or *Purity*. Yet, to the makers of the book, this was the most important of all. The faith must be kept to the last and final degree, the law observed to its jot and tittle, the Jewish people segregated from the corruption of the gentile world. Once this principle of integrity be accepted then these otherwise extraordinary regulations as to mixed seeds, animals and materials (verses 9 to 11) make rather more sense. Yet there is, maybe, for us a deeper meaning. We are so skilful at manipulation, so ready to cross-fertilise and experiment, that we can forget that everything has its own individual nature and quality. Is it really according to the nature of the hen that we breed it in batteries and turn its parturition-process into a production line? Or to the nature of the calf, that we keep it in darkness to fatten, in anaemia to whiten, its meat? Is it possible to be so forgetful of the individual rights of all other creatures that in the end we forget those of man? Have nations and cultural communities their own individual right to survive and their special contribution to make? Is it possible to be so absorbed with mankind that we forget man is always an individual? Britain has a traditional affection for its eccentrics : maybe this is something we do well to cherish and preserve.

30

THE LEGACY OF MOSES

EVERY FAMILIAR NAME HAS AS its counterpart a mental picture. In the case of Moses, this picture, for most of us, is that of an imposing bearded figure frowning upon the people whom he dominates. Yet, in the forming of this concept, we have been more influenced by Michaelangelo and other eminent artists than by the actual story itself.

For Moses was, above all things, a man of deep personal humility and warm affection. He was distrustful of his own abilities, apt to overwork and to overworry (the really self-sufficient have, like Napoleon, the power of switching off their concentration at will), and totally committed in affection to an often extremely ungrateful people. He experienced, in fact, everything that usually falls to the lot of the devoted politician or reformer. But he was also, it is clear, a man of considerable personal charm. He took endless trouble with his subordinates and was always ready to give credit and responsibility alike to those who deserved them. His life is an admirable illustration of the fact that a man can usually get any job through, any reform accomplished, if he is only concerned with the need to get the work *done,* and not with the desire that it should be known to be done by *him.*

Indeed, the final scene in Moses' life is proof of this. At long last the people of Israel have come to their journey's end. Now for the flags and the shouting, the titles and decorations. Now for honoured retirement and honorary degrees. But no, even these very real delights are to be denied him. He will be left behind, as the nation goes forward. He must be content with the fact that he has done his work. It seems a hard judgment upon a great man. Yet it is also the final mark of greatness. His work has been done for its own sake and not for any honour or recognition it can bring him. It is work done, that is, for God.

Once before Moses showed this same total commitment. It

was the occasion when his people had been more than usually stupid and stubborn, and Moses feared that this time they really had gone beyond forgiveness. But he was still prepared to plead their case, and to identify himself totally with them.

There is about the life of Moses, the leader of his people, a great deal that anticipates the life of Christ himself. He stands, as Christ does, between man and God, interpreting God to man and interceding for man with God. He is endlessly — or in Moses' case, almost endlessly — patient, greatly loved yet essentially lonely. He uses and delegates power, yet is never obsessed by it. As the vivid and poetic language of the Bible asserts, "his face shone" : this borrowed glory must, his people believed, be a reflection of the divine glory; he must have "seen God" — if not face to face, yet in the splendour of his being. Moses' life deserves our study; Jewish history is his epitaph.

JOSHUA 2

31

RAHAB THE HARLOT

THE CITY OF JERICHO COMMANDS the ford of Jordan. It is the key to that mountain road to Jerusalem by which Judea is approached from the east and along which the Good Samaritan jogged to find the victim of a road accident prostrate in the ditch. Joshua, an able military commander, sends his scouts in disguise to discover the possibilities of taking Jericho, either by violence or by craft.

They find lodging with a prostitute named Rahab, but are betrayed, and a posse is sent to arrest them. Their temporary hostess hides them beneath the flax laid out to dry on the flat roof — as many a fugitive has been hidden in the hay of a barn — and misleads the police. She then smuggles the spies out in the same way as St. Paul escaped from Damascus; in return, they promise her immunity. Her house is to be distinguished, when the general attack is made, by a scarlet thread or "clew" (this has given its name to the distinguishing "clue" of our detective stories). A "disorderly house" was a sensible choice for any under-cover men. Strange men coming and going at odd hours would not, they might suppose, attract attention, nor would its inhabitants be on such terms with the authorities as to give away doubtful visitors.

These ideas, in the main, proved right. Rahab not only saved their lives, but gave invaluable information as to the "alarm and despondency" on which the invader could rely — evidence of the importance of propaganda in any campaign.

How far should we consider her conduct as treachery? How far indeed do we believe that the nation or community has any demands of loyalty on an individual whom it has itself condemned as an outcast?

This is a problem which war intensifies and underlines; it also links it with that of the man or woman who, genuinely believing his or her country to be in the wrong, sells its secrets to the enemy. We, acting as a community anxious to survive, send such people to gaol or firing squad; history sometimes regards them as martyrs to truth. Rahab herself later married into a respectable Jewish family, became the mother of a Biblical hero — Boaz — and is recorded as an ancestress of Christ himself (Matthew 1, verse 5).

She also takes her place in that gallery of golden-hearted prostitutes, which includes *La Dâme aux Camélias* and Maupassant's *Boule de Suif* along with the heroines of *Never on Sunday* and *Rattle of a Simple Man*. Is there some sense of guilt, a recognition that it is demand which creates supply, that makes us anxious to believe that the paid apparatus of sexual desire may still involve genuine and compassionate love? Or is it a recognition that there are in fact worse sins than physical ones, an idea which Christ taught but which we are on the whole reluctant to accept?

32

PROPAGANDA CAMPAIGN

WE SOMETIMES TALK AS THOUGH it were only in our own time that success in battle or revolution had depended upon possession of weapons at least as much as on right or on courage. This is, of course, nonsense. Throughout history battles have been won by the combination of superior equipment, intelligent command, and trained and enthusiastic fighting men. No single item alone ensures success — though occasionally one of them, by itself, obtains it.

Now the Hebrew forces, entering Canaan from the east across the Jordan valley, found themselves confronted with an obstacle entirely new to them — a walled city. They had neither such machines as had then been devised for reducing fortifications — nor yet the experience of investing cities by counter-fortification. Even methods of river-crossing by ford or dam had been seemingly unknown to them. What then could they do? Impossible to take the mountain road and leave Jericho in its palm groves on flank and rear — and impossible, also, to bring its people to battle.

However, in Joshua the invaders had an outstanding general, as story after story proves to us. He first surrounded the city, cutting off all supply and communication. Next, he produced a remarkable plan.

Day after day, for six days, the army marched in silence once round the city, its band playing. Then on the seventh day, they repeated the circuit seven times — and at the end of the last circuit made a sudden demonstration.

What happened? Some archaeologists, examining the ruins of early Jericho, claim that there is evidence for an earthquake : other historians suggest that fire and scaling ladders did all that was needed. The real miracle, of course, is not whether or not the top-heavy walls of baked clay did or did not fall down flat at a given moment — but that the apparently impossible came true. A Bedouin horde, without experience or siege trains, stormed a heavily defended city without serious opposition. The mysterious activities of the host somehow sapped the courage of the citizens, whilst the investment of the walls cut off the possibility of messengers obtaining help from outside.

Equally, these same mysterious activities evidently had their psychological effect on the morale of the attackers, quite apart from the opportunity they gave of examining the fortifications and the strength of their garrison. To the actual participants, perhaps, they further represented the condemnation of the city, the imposing of a religious "ban" upon it.

And that suggests to us that there is no situation which need be considered hopeless. Many a fight has been won by a boxer, almost out on his feet, remembering that his opponent is probably feeling just as tired. And the mere fact that the enemy takes a defensive attitude and relies on the protection of walls rather than on his own fighting spirit suggests that he is already beaten in his heart. Joshua wears down the morale of Jericho — and then commits his forces to a single and decisive blow. He did this because he was a man of faith, as well as of courage. And, whatever the mechanism involved — it worked. When in doubt — take the initiative. When afraid, sally out against the enemy. The man who maintains the defensive is a man already half-beaten, since he has admitted in his heart that the enemy is, on level terms, the stronger party.

JUDGES 4. 13–24

33

WHEN IS A CRIME NOT A CRIME?

THE DOMINANT INFLUENCES IN military history are of two sorts — great generals and new inventions. When they coincide, the world reels. Thus, for centuries the chariot was master of the field. It failed at last, against the mobile fortress of the phalanx and the locked shields of the legion. This supremacy in turn was challenged by the speed and fire-power of mounted archers, themselves superseded, once the stirrup was invented and a man could strike from his horse's back without risk of falling-off, by the armed knight. All these weapons were used — often with original variations — by the masters of battle.

Now this chapter begins, after the assassination of King Ehud in the latrine had temporarily set Israel free, with the powerful combination of fighting chariots and a capable general, which resulted in Israel's virtual enslavement.

But they had a "seer", a wise woman named Deborah, to whom people came with their troubles and problems, and she selected a capable young man named Barak to lead an insurrection. He is modest, as well as capable, and insists that she shall accompany him. But he finds it difficult to raise a fighting force. Chapter 5 describes the unwillingness of the shepherds and fishermen to join it, perhaps because, as the same chapter emphasises, they were practically without military equipment.

However, they entice the enemy's massive chariots into rough going, and a sudden and tremendous rainstorm (see chapter 5, verses 4 and 21) makes these useless and mutually encumbering. Their general flies on foot, and seeks refuge in the tent of a nomad Bedouin, whose friend he was. The master of the tent is away, but his wife takes in the tired soldier, makes much of him, and waits till he is asleep. Then she murders him with tent-peg and mallet.

Many attempts have been made to whitewash this crime against all the decent laws of kinship and hospitality. It has been suggested that the weary man was asleep within the women's quarters and that this, if discovered by Heber himself, would have meant death to Jael.

But it is quite clear that her contemporaries had no such idea. To them she was like any heroine of the Resistance who beguiled and poisoned a Gestapo officer. This man, maybe for some reason of blood-feud or because she was of Israelite stock, was the arch enemy of her people. He had lorded it over them through the chance that he had chariots and they had none. Now it happened that she had the weapons and he was helpless. Must she hold her hand and see Israel again enslaved? Or strike and let them go free?

What should we have done if we had been in her place? What is the duty of the individual who may have it in his power to save a nation at the cost of personal deceit? Can we be convicted of selfishness in valuing our personal integrity above the needs and safety of other people? Should we be prepared to lie if by doing it we could help an innocent victim? Was Deborah right in calling Jael "blessed above women"? Indeed, if we had happened to be Philistines, should we have felt the same about Delilah? Just where do public loyalty and personal integrity begin and end? It is easy to indulge in private moral scruples if one is both free and safe. Indeed, it has been suggested for this very reason that morality is the invention of those who *are* free and safe, to inhibit the slaves from rebellion. How much of moral judgement as to the wrongs of industrial direct-action (the kind which most threatens our own security) proceeds from an economic rather than religious basis?

JUDGES 6. 11–40

34

ICONOCLASM AND COMMON-SENSE

THE BOOK OF JUDGES CONTAINS two remarkable family situations — one of tragic frustration, as we shall see later, and one of admirable common-sense. This particular family (the latter example) were poor farmers in the tribe of Manasseh, whose settlements straddled the North Jordan Valley and were open to desert raiders. A combination of these, with their swift riding-camels, and of regular troops from Amalek, had devastated the country and driven the Israelites to take refuge as outlaws in the woods and rocky heights, where they could secretly scratch a living. Even corn must be threshed under cover, for fear the flying chaff, like chimney-smoke, should give away their guerilla hide-out.

So word comes to the youngest son, evidently a powerfully built young man, that he is to call the people to arms. Encouraged by a sign of divine favour, he is told to start by putting to rights his own family-worship. This is a most dangerous demand, since it involves, amongst other things, killing off the best of his father's few cattle, but he collects some of his friends and in the dark of the night the deed is done.

When it is discovered, there is trouble. His death is demanded and it is here that his father, Joash, comes into his own. He has the tough common-sense of his son. Like him, he is not easily to be stampeded or persuaded. All right, he says, fair enough. If this God, whose altar my son has destroyed, is a real god, let him do something about it himself. Leave it to him to prove his case.

So Gideon's life is saved — but he is a cautious man. He wants further proof of his mission. Let a fleece, laid out on the ground all night, be wet in the morning and the soil dry: that will do. This is granted, but he thinks again. It's not so difficult for moisture to condense in an absorbent substance, as we all know. But much harder to explain, if the *ground* is wet and the *fleece* is dry. God, one is inclined to feel, is pleased with the experimental approach of the young scientist — and in the next chapter, well worth reading for its own sake, his scientific approach is applied to warfare.

In the first place, he deliberately whittles down his striking force to a mere handful of volunteers. In the second, he puts them to some sort of test of suitability. (Possibly those who "lapped" from the hand were men who kept on the alert whilst drinking: the others, thinking only of thirst, left themselves defenceless whilst prone beside the water. Or the first group may have drunk in moderation, the second without restraint.)

Finally, the tiny army employ all the techniques of "psychological warfare". First, they discover that there is some degree of alarm and despondency among the enemy troops: then, they follow it up with a night attack so dramatically staged that the whole force panics and commits a kind of corporate hara-kiri.

The rest of the story is not quite so happy. But it is an interesting lesson in "man-management": see how differently Gideon deals, for instance, with the men of Ephraim and with the churlish "princes of Succoth". A strong man and a strong ruler, the country was in peace while he lived. But his concubine-borne son, who might be called "Fitzgideon", was to cause grim tragedy after his death. We, who treat illegitimacy so lightly, might well consider from the Bible, if not from Shakespeare, how dark a shadow it can sometimes cast upon the children who are born out of wedlock. To feel oneself in any sense unwanted is to develop a truculence, a determination to make the world accept us, whether it likes it or not. To be secure in mind is usually to be peaceable in behaviour.

JUDGES 11. 29–40

35

JEPHTHAH'S BAD BARGAIN

How many Bible stories are concerned with promises! Specially with promises — or oaths — whose keeping involved the maker in unexpected and disagreeable results. Our own reaction to Jephthah is one of horror. How could a father think it right to keep such a promise? Why didn't his daughter run away?

Yet the person who urges that the vow must be kept is the daughter herself. The keeping of it is regarded as a moral obligation—as it was for King Darius (in the case of Daniel) or for Herod as regards John Baptist. There are two evident reasons for this. The first, that of the covenant or bargain. The whole of Jewish history was built upon this concept of sacred agreement. God had solemnly pledged himself to care for his people so long as they remained faithful to him.

Circumcision was the outward seal of this bargain — as the rainbow was the pledge of returning spring. Prophets might enlarge upon and modify the nature of the covenant, but it still remained the "Old Testament", until a new promise was made and a "New Testament" delivered, attested by blood, and accepted by the new Israel with the seal of baptism.

To break a bargain was, therefore, to sin against God, as is implied surely by the Third Commandment. Once God's name is invoked to an oath it is absolute and binding. No one has the right to contract out of it because it doesn't pay as he expected, or because the terms are onerous. This was accepted as true of human business deals, and became the solid base of commerce. No nation can develop an advanced economic system without some recognition of the "sacredness" of agreements at a commercial level: no nation is likely to command much respect internationally unless it honours its pledged word.

Second, if it was important that everyone should "keep his word, though it were to his own hindrance", it was even more important that kings and judges should do so. Since their power was in practice absolute, limited only by the code of law obtaining in their country ("the law of the Medes and Persians" or whatever it might be), it was essential that their pledged word should be inviolate. Without this, all authority must come to an end, since authority *was*, in fact, the royal word expressed through his vice-gerents and representatives. For a great personage to forswear himself was to challenge the whole basis of authority and so to threaten it. No monarch could afford to do this without questioning his own right to rule.

Jephthah had made a direct agreement with God: God had, as Jephthah saw it, kept to his side of the bargain. How *could* he, brought up as he was in the story of Abraham and Isaac, withdraw just because the cost was far above anything he had expected?

What parallel does our own experience offer? It is difficult to find one, in that we have largely lost respect for agreements. Governments denounce treaties made by a previous party in power, or refuse to honour their own election pledges on the ground that it is no longer expedient to do so. Commercial companies explain away their apparent guarantees: the "promise to pay" of banknotes is evaded by depreciating currency.

Perhaps the nearest we ever come to the Jephthah situation is in those cases where a man, in order to honour commitments or to meet the needs of a business for which he holds himself morally responsible, pledges all the family's resources and thereby

78

impoverishes them. But this is so infrequent as to sound fictional : he is far more likely, so as to safeguard himself at the cost of the business, to put everything he possibly can into his wife's name ! Both to Jephthah and to his daughter the family honour was sacred, and each member of the family was involved in its maintenance. There is genuine nobility in this sense of obligation.

36

STRENGTH GONE TO WASTE

COMPARED WITH THE STORY OF Gideon, the story of Samson is a sad one. Immensely gifted (after all, vast physical strength is just as much of a gift as a vast intellect), capable of leading the people into freedom, he wasted his powers by using them in self-interest, was the fool of any astute woman who cared to exploit him and ended, like many another lethal weapon, in a destructive explosion.

Unlike many strong men, he was quick-tempered, and, once he went berserk, quite impossible to control. Yet the story of his birth is a most moving one, and evidence for the kind of man he might have been — and the kind of good he might have done — if only he had ever learned self-discipline. Is it possible that the parents were so proud of the gifted son, born, it seemed miraculously, when they had lost hope of a family, that they spoiled him thoroughly? (Chapter 14, verse 3 suggests a boy who had never been denied anything he wanted.)

Yet his parents were both devout, and anxious to do right. His mother learns, as Mary the Virgin was to do, by special intimation that she is to bear a child. He is to be devoted to God, like Samuel and John the Baptist : like them, this special loyalty is to be expressed in abstinence from alcohol and in un-shorn hair — as though they were to be completely and totally "natural", left altogether and entirely to be as God would make and use them.

And his father is very anxious that they shall do their part as good parents. Perhaps he was too anxious : perhaps something of a nervous and flustered little man, dreadfully afraid of doing and saying the wrong thing, almost too fulsomely polite to the stranger — and correspondingly frightened when he discovered his true nature. It is here that the splendid common-sense of his wife comes into the picture. Whilst he is dithering in apprehension, she gets on, one may suppose, with the washing-up, commenting only that God would scarcely have given them all these exciting plans and delightful possibilities if he meant them to drop dead next moment.

Unhappily, Manoah's devout anxiety and his wife's sturdy common-sense were not enough. The child of their pride and joy became a seven-days' wonder and not a hero of God. No good home, no strong inheritance of blood, no extraordinary endowment of birth can compel a man to fulfil the purpose of his being. He is free to accept or reject, to use his powers in the service of other people — or to spend them on his own gratification.

The story of Samson is a reminder of man's absolute freedom to reject the divine purpose, as well as to collaborate with it. The gifts he might have used to save his nation and to re-establish it in dignity were frittered away in self-indulgence — whose consequences were borne by others than himself. It is an unhappy comment upon our attitude towards reality that for one person who knows of Gideon, ten are familiar with Samson — and this is true of church — as well as of film-goers.

RUTH I. I–I8

37

MOTHER-IN-LAW

IF THERE WAS ONE NATION THAT the people of Israel really disliked (and, in fact, there were very many such), it was the Moabites. These were Bedouin, living in the hills and deserts on the east of the Jordan, natural enemies of a farming people. Perhaps the bad feeling was made worse because the Israelites had once been nomads and wanderers themselves, and felt a secret envy of the freedom of the men of Moab. At all events, they lived on terms rather like those of the English and Scots in the time of the cattle-raiders. There was a great fear on the part of the settled farmers, and a contempt on that of the raiders. One can compare, perhaps, the sentiments of Red Indians and frontiersmen as the west developed?

But, as always happens when people are neighbours, some dare to cross the border, whether for adventure, friendship, commerce — or for sheer need. It was hunger that drove a citizen of Bethlehem, with his wife and two sons. But they found, as we usually do, that the hated and feared enemy turned out to be a person much like themselves, and then they settled down so successfully that, when the father of the family died, the two boys married locally and lived happily, not indeed for ever after, but for ten peaceful years. Then they died too, and Naomi the widowed mother determined to go home. She knew that the famine that made them emigrate was over, and that there would be a place for her with her own folk.

Her two daughters-in-law went with her to the frontier where she said goodbye. Both at first refused to leave her, but she turned away their entreaties with a sad little joke. By Jewish law and custom, a younger son would marry his dead brother's widow so as to assure her of a home. Could she, she said, at *her* time of life bear more sons? And could they wait till the babies were grown into men?

So one of the girls kissed her and said goodbye: the other, Ruth, went on with Naomi, went on, as the rest of the book tells, to marry very successfully and to become in due course one of the ancestresses of Christ.

One of the interests of this romantic little story is that such "foreign" marriage was extremely unpopular with the Israelites. They believed that foreign wives not only tainted the stock of their own people, but very often brought with them foreign gods and a corrupting faith. Nehemiah, for instance, ruthlessly split up every single such marriage that he encountered among his people. Yet the editors who included in the Bible the racial Puritanism of Nehemiah were prepared to accept

81

Ruth and to admit her to the blood-line of the ancestors of David — rather as though Dr. Verwoerd were to announce cheerfully that his great-grandmother had been a Hottentot. But racial intermarriage is a fact which we have to face — and it is quite clear that we need to think out our reaction to it carefully and without passion.

What are the arguments against it? Very largely they arise from our own social and personal failures. It is not the marriage that is difficult so much as the way the rest of us react to it. Of *course* it is hard for two people of different racial tradition to suit their lives to each other; but perhaps not as hard as for two people of widely different temperament — or taste — or education. We have seen in the public life of our time, as well as in the private experience of many of us, plenty of cases of extraordinarily happy, fulfilled, and valuable marriages between people of totally different race and colour.

Too often, our own minds are conditioned by the imperialist background of the white races. We think of black and brown people as servants and inferiors, whose women were taken to the beds of their European masters, and whose men were treated permanently as "boys", immature beings — whilst, in the coverts of the subconscious, they were envied as the possessors of supposedly immense virility.

The story of Ruth is the story of a girl of tremendous character and loyalty, a girl in whom love — first for her husband and then for her husband's mother — overcame all the natural barriers of race, tradition, and even religion. She was ready to leave behind her every security and familiarity for the sake of an alien mother-in-law. Such women are of the stock of the great pioneers : Boaz was a wise man to recognise her quality.

I Samuel 3. 1–18

38

A LONELY CHILD

A CURLY-HAIRED CHILD, IN A clean white nightgown, sitting up in bed with an expression of pious appreciation — the picture is dreadfully familiar to us from the books pressed on us in childhood. It is, however, a polite travesty of the original story, a fig-leaf over the facts of a stark situation.

What are these facts? An older woman longing for a child, to justify her existence, to prove to a mocking world, summed up in her fruitful co-wife, that she too is a woman, with all a woman's capacities. In return for this justification she will surrender her rights and responsibilities, and the child shall be brought up as a temple acolyte. Or rather, she will "lend" the child. This is a strange phrase which may possibly suggest belief in a life after death, but may also indicate the idea of a bargain between Hannah and God, later fully implemented when, in place of Samuel, she had three sons and two daughters.

The boy grows up in a strange and unhappy world. The priest-family who not only look after the temple but act as the channels of communication with divinity are themselves corrupt. The word that should come through them therefore dries up — there is no vision, and the people perish.

But, when the official channel dries up, springs leap out elsewhere. A wandering "man of God" brings word to Eli that judgement has gone out against him. The muttering indignation of the whole people is focussed in this one selected instance — one, doubtless, of an increasing series. And then — the climax. Final doom pronounced by a child. The curly-haired infant of the popular picture is not an infant babbling gratitude for a kitten, but condemning a man to death.

Do we find this thought so repulsive that we shy away from it, and retreat into sentimental convention? Only if we refuse to admit the fact that millions of children do have to face moral choice and to make decisions just as important as Samuel's.

We may suppose him to have been a boy — as he certainly became a man — of immense moral strength. He grows up in what should have been a centre of righteousness, the home of honour and integrity. Instead, he finds dishonesty and corruption, sometimes cynical and sometimes hypocritical. He must have hated it, yet his fire is damped down both by affection for the old weakling, Eli, and by a sense of obedience and respect.

Then, as he grows older, he becomes aware that he is not alone in his indignation : he sees the sacrifices despoiled and the faith of the people cheated. And so he realises not only that judgement is gone out against the family of Eli, but that he is called to accept personal responsibility within the situation. In fact, he grows up, since to accept one's share of responsibility is to become an adult. That in his case the load is a heavy one, since it seems to involve cutting his one remaining bond of affection, is secondary to the basic truth. His situation is really that of the eleven-year-old girl who looks after a flock of brothers and sisters, whilst her widowed mother goes out to work, or that of the adolescent boy who stands up in defence of his mother against a drunken father. God is no more a respecter of age than of persons. When there is a capacity for moral response the demand is made upon it.

Perhaps, though, there was a price to be paid. The later life of Samuel is that of a man married to his job, a man who sometimes seems without compassion. Taken as an infant from his parents, for reasons incomprehensible to a child, brought up as a "devotee", a person loaned to God, finding that his childish affections had then been given to a man without moral worth, no wonder the adult Samuel became lonely, self-sufficient, fanatic. May be it was such a one-track personality who was needed to pilot his people through the stormy waters ahead of them — a man who could hear a call through the darkness and answer it without counting the cost.

1 SAMUEL 4. 3–11 and compare 6. 1–16

39

TOTEM AND TABOO

WE HAVE, ON THE WHOLE, QUITE lost the idea of what anthropologists call "mana", the sense of a special and potent holiness to be associated with particular objects and places. About the nearest we get to it is in ghost-stories, or in the belief that it is "lucky" to drink of this well, or to touch that stone.

But earlier peoples were quite certain that there were good places — to which the sensible made pilgrimage to acquire some of that goodness — and bad ones, to be avoided. There were objects, too, which were helpful — "totems"; or dangerous and forbidden — "taboos". Different nations and even different tribes or blood groups had different totems and taboos, and it was very important to get them right. Some objects, indeed, could be both "totem" and "taboo". They were holy and significant, but they must be treated with the utmost respect.

For the Israelites, the greatest of these was the Ark. This was a wooden chest, guarded by two heraldic or angelic winged beings, and containing within it a sort of potted history of the nation. It was regarded as the seat or throne of God, and also as the repository of his glory. Where the Ark was, there was the power of God.

Now in the ordinary way the Ark was kept in safety, first within the tabernacle, the tent-church of the forty years' journey, later at a suitable centre, and ultimately in the temple at Jerusalem, until this was destroyed in A.D. 70, and the contents of the Ark carried off to Rome, where they disappeared.

In times of crisis it could be brought out to show the people that their God was visibly with them. It happened so on this occasion. Unfortunately, in spite of the borrowed self-confidence of Israel, in spite of the superstitious apprehension of the Philistine — it did not work. Israel was defeated again, and the Ark captured — only to prove so troublesome a prize that it was in the end repatriated, and that not without calamity.

What went wrong? The very simple fact that God was *not* with Israel, and that they were *not* fighting for him but simply for themselves. The story is a useful reminder that it is not always those who profess to represent the "Christian point of view" or to support its "eternal values" who are really on the right side at all. There is a moment when it is better to quit oneself like a man and *fight* than it is to make pious and pompous claims as to one's divine authority and await heavenly interference. God, as chapter 6 in its primitive way suggests, is

perfectly well able to look after himself. Those who are anxious
to defend Christendom against what they regard as the "Worse-
than-Death" of other political creeds may not find their own
particular Ark an infallible guarantee of success. God does not
automatically and immediately support those who like to call
upon him — or to be called by his name. The label on a cause
is not a guarantee either of its success or of its justification.

1 SAMUEL 16

40

DAVID, MAN AND MONARCH

DAVID IS ONE OF THE MOST
fascinating characters of the Bible. "Fascinating" is right. He
has an overwhelming charm, mixed with a patient sagacity that
enables him not only to get on terms with everyone he comes
across, man or woman, but to get out of them whatever he
wants. The whole of his extraordinary life is evidence of this. A
country boy, retaining a precarious place at court; an outlaw,
with a price on his head, always hunted, never betrayed; an
exile, prevailing on foreign kings by sheer intelligence; a ruling
monarch, conciliating his enemies; an old man, expelled by his
own son — in each varied situation, he still contrives to hold
the affection of his friends and even to win over his enemies.

In spite of this, he is essentially a lonely man, looking for love
and enjoying it, but in his heart, solitary. The psalms, which
must at least in some part be his work, are evidence of this. In
his charm, his wisdom, even in his solitariness, he anticipates his
mighty Descendant.

Anyone interested in "man-management" should study the
life-history of this extraordinary man. Notice the ingenuity with
which he gets his project to the king's notice (chapter 17, verses
30, 31): in no time he is at home in the royal family, without
losing any of his general popularity. It was presumably this
popularity that enabled him to be so well-informed about Saul's

murderous plots, helped as he was in addition both by his wife and his brother-in-law. Humble people were always on his side, and even Philistines and Moabites could not resist him. The tough old soldier Abner; Abner's slayer, the even tougher soldier, Joab; eighty-year-old Barzillai; the prophets Nathan and Gad who were foremost to rebuke him — all seem to have felt this extraordinary love-attracting quality. It was partly, we may suppose, his generosity in forgiveness, partly, his readiness to admit a fault: but charm cannot be explained, only accepted.

It must also be realised that charm is a quality of great danger. It is power, and power can be used for good or bad. It is badly used, when it is used for a man's own self-centred purposes, so that people are treated as "means" and manipulated to produce desired results. It is well used, when it is subservient to a great purpose, and only employed to encourage others to discover in themselves the ability to respond to that purpose. A good personality helps people to become their own best selves — and they will respond with gratitude and trust. A bad personality imposes itself on others, whether through exploiting their weakness or through dazzling their susceptibility. Such "charm" in the end defeats itself, for the holder comes to rely upon it and upon nothing else — and it is a weapon that one day breaks in his hand.

I SAMUEL 17. 17–52

41

THE CHAMP

OUR SYMPATHIES ARE ALWAYS with the Little Man against the Big one. This isn't just because we little men must stick together if we're not to be bullied by the big ones. Part, at least, of our feeling is due to our sense of fair play — which turns us against the bully — and of "poetic justice". "Poetic justice" simply means that occasionally right will overcome might — and this suggests a power other than a material one, which sometimes comes to the aid of the under-dog. "Poetic justice", then, in the sense of "artificial" or "created" justice, is life turning out as it ought to be and not as it is.

This is why the story of David and Goliath gives us so much pleasure. For David is a real fairy-story hero. He is young, a "stripling" (but much more than Barrie's or Bergner's "boy": after all, he *had* killed a lion and a bear hand-to-hand, or hand-to-paw). He is handsome. He is brave. He has a fine turn of speech. He is also a crack marksman. He goes out to fight a braggart and a bully — and he wins.

But if we turn aside from the deep satisfaction of Little-Man-beating-Big-Man, there is a real interest in this whole idea of solving national disputes by the conflict of individual champions. We recognise this emotionally rather than intellectually. For instance, people who regard Christian belief as to Christ's identi-fication of himself, the "Son of Man", with the whole human race — and with all that this implies — as irrational nonsense, will at the same time get wildly excited over a boxer or a foot-ball team who are representing Britain. It is almost impossible to watch a wrestling match on T.V., or a village cricket team, without finding oneself "taking sides". And this means wanting *our* team to win.

The "champion" is therefore the incarnation of his people's hopes. He represents them, faces danger on their behalf. We see this today in, for example, Westerns. Over and again the hero is the man who, like David, appears unexpectedly. He rides into town, discovers that everyone in town is puzzled by a mystery or terrorised by fear, shoots it out (again like David, first of the quick-drawing gunmen), and is at once made their champion (elected sheriff). The only difference is that Westerns must go on and on, so the hero has to ride away into the sunset to repeat his exploits somewhere else next Saturday.

Is there, in all this, some faint anticipation of the work of Christ? He too comes from the unknown into the situation. He too makes others' cares his own. He too fights it out to the death — in this case, his own death. He, like David, thereby earns a kingdom, though — like the Western hero — he hands back responsibility to the people on the spot. No giant was ever so dreaded as Death, no villain ever so wicked as Christ's opponent — but it is a fight *à l'outrance,* a duel to the end, none the less. Little men, we need a champion still.

I SAMUEL 20

42

THE DEMON SEX AGAIN?

ONE OF THE DIFFICULTIES OF OUR present age is that any friendship between people of the same sex is instantly suspect. We detect incipient homosexuality in all relationships, irrespective of age and disposition, and apparently without any consideration for the absence of physical manifestation. Such absence, we decide, is a sign of "repression" — and the case is all the more clearly proven.

But those periods of history which have been most fully aware of the emotional possibilities of homosexual relationship have also been the richest in every kind and shade of friendship. They have recognised that emotion must of course have its part in all friendship, but that this emotion is not necessarily expressed in feelings of desire or possession. It may simply be a sensation of pleasure in another's company, which, when enriched by a sense of shared interest and similar — or complementary — opinions and interests, leads to a stable and agreeable intimacy.

But, come to that, when does friendship of this normal and admirable sort pass over into a relationship which deserves condemnation? What are the elements of homosexualism which we condemn? Are they, for instance, the very qualities we admire in heterosexual monogamy, the choice of one person to be a permanent partner, and the preferring of that person above all others? Is the jealousy of the homosexual monstrous, the mutual absorption of the happily married honourable?

Can we admit "homosexual" partnerships as permissible, if they abstain from extremes of physical expression? And, if it is physical expression that is the evil, does homosexual friendship between a couple become permissible once passion is spent and affection takes its place?

On the whole, the characteristics of homosexualism which we condemn are those which we find equally unworthy in the heterosexual — as, for instance, possessive jealousy, domineering and dominating love, commercial prostitution, and the corruption of youth.

The story of David and Jonathan may be — and sometimes has been — claimed as a story of homosexual passion. But it may be no less a story of ordinary human friendship. In military campaigning soldiers strike up a particular form of comradeship with a fellow soldier, a comradeship which is deepened by a sense of mutual dependency and mutual peril. But this is as common between the fiercely heterosexual as between the doubtfully homosexual. The friendship of David and Jonathan seems to have been of this sort. It was without trace of jealousy: indeed, one of its most attractive features is the utter refusal of Jonathan to feel himself overshadowed or diminished by the exploits of his friend. Loyal to his father even when this brought his own life to disaster, he was loyal, too, to his friend.

So David, in the magnificent lament of the second reference above, makes no distinction between his friend and his enemy. He loves and admires them both, and sees the best not only in their nature but in their tragic history. No one, reading this, can honestly claim that he was "in love" with one, but emotionally unaware of the other. Nor yet, surely, that this is a sort of homosexual incest, when he loved both generations at once. Nor yet looking at the rest of his life, that David was a homosexual, incapable of satisfying relationships with women.

It is simpler — and a good deal more honest — to admit that men and women can find satisfaction and stimulus in friendship with their own sex, just as they can in friendship with the other. And they can do it without necessarily falling victims to the power of Venus.

43

THE CLEVERNESS OF ABIGAIL

EVERYONE — OR ALMOST EVERY-
one — knows about David and Goliath. Their situation is part
of folk history and has been expressed for an age — and perhaps
for many ages to come — in the image of Charlie Chaplin. But
the story of Abigail is almost equally fascinating — Abigail, one
of the three remarkable women in David's life. Like Bathsheba,
she was beautiful. She was also highly intelligent. Like Michal,
she came from an aristocratic background. In Abigail's case, her
aristocracy was of wealth. She came of the landed gentry and
was married to Nabal, a surly alcoholic, whose money had only
made him obstinate and overbearing. David is living "on the
country" — as a bandit — and he needs maintenance. So he
sends to ask, politely, for what is really "protection money".
We've laid off you, says the message — how about a little something in return? And as Nabal's own people admit, real protection it has been. The reply is an offensive snub. A runaway slave,
of no family (here speaks the snob), presuming to ask for recognition? Not on your life.

David decides on immediate action. He equips a raiding force
and sets out. But Abigail is a much better — or a much wiser —
character than this husband of hers. She loads up a really handsome gift, necessities and luxuries both, and hurries off without
telling her husband. And when she meets David, she talks him
round as cleverly as he would have done in a like situation
himself.

Please, she says, pay no attention to my stupid and unimportant husband — it's all my fault, but it wasn't intended. You're
destined for greatness, I know, and once you're as successful as
you will be, you won't want to think that you took it out on us
for our ignorance and folly. And, please, in days to come, don't
forget me.

A plea like this, from a beautiful woman in tears, would soften most hearts, let alone one as susceptible as David's. Of course he gave in at once.

Then follows the subtle vengeance of Abigail on her brute of a husband. While he is in the throes of a hangover after one of his usual debauches she tells him that he is only alive to enjoy it because she, a woman, his wife, has gone suppliant to the upstart outlaw and has bribed him with the best the house contained. Nabal cannot bear it: he has an immediate stroke: he is paralysed for ten days, and dies. So she marries David and if she does not live happy ever after, at least lives to enjoy an exciting and unusual life.

Oriental tradition may have denied normal human rights to a woman, but it is remarkable how sheer ability, specially when linked with remarkable beauty, can make nonsense of human social limitations. Abigail is, in her own right, one of the outstanding women of the Bible.

I SAMUEL 28. 3–25

44

A KINDLY MEDIUM
(THE WITCH OF ENDOR)

THE PRACTICE OF SPIRITUALISM is a very old one, and existed long before spirit rappings were recorded near Rochester, N.Y., a hundred years ago.

It has always contained two elements. There is *curiosity*: what *does* happen when we are dead? along, no doubt, with a desire for reassurance that it is going to be all right. And there is a *wish for power*. If I could know the future, I could prepare for it — and I should have an advantage over those who don't and can't.

Sincere and devoted spiritualists are concerned with the first of these; but a high proportion of those who attend seances do so to get useful advice as to their activities, whether in terms of domestic life or of business enterprises.

There is always, too, an element of *self-importance,* of being one of those in the know. The life of that extraordinary man, Alisteir Crowley, is a case in point. How much he wanted to "matter", how much he and his like pride themselves on being initiates, persons of power — even if that power is wholly and admittedly evil. Worst of all, it turns out to be ineffective. The tragedy of a witch is the spells that don't work, the enemy who stubbornly refuses to turn into a toad, the broomstick that never takes off.

Black magic is, of course, primarily the supposed technique of obtaining power, by drawing it from occult sources. When these sources are associated with the spirits of the dead (rather than with "evil spirits", intelligences that are non-human) it passes over into spiritualism, and the witch becomes a "medium".

The witch or wizard has, or claims to have, the ability to control and compel spirits, human or inhuman. The medium is, as the name suggests, merely a person whose alleged particular gift is one of maintaining communication between the two worlds, material and spiritual, the Here and the Hereafter. Saul, in the days of his glory, had suppressed all witches and mediums, all those, in fact, who tried to foretell the future except through the accepted channels of prophecy, of visions, and of "Urim". (This was some sort of official technique of religious divination used by the priests.)

Now, lonely, embittered, afraid, he turns in despair to the methods he had despised, as Hitler turned to fortune-tellers.

Eventually a practitioner is found, and the seance proceeds according to convention. A spirit is summoned and pronounces no message of hope, not even an oracle of double-meaning which could be interpreted for present comfort — but only forecast of doom. Saul is overcome, but the woman (which is what the Bible calls her : "witch" is the description in the English headings only) out of pity nurses, feeds, and restores him.

But what about the apparition? Is it genuine? Are we really to suppose that the techniques of an experienced medium are all that is wanted to summon to us the souls of the dead? Quite apart from the morality — or the impertinence — of so doing, is it effective? "I can call spirits from the mighty deep" says

Glendower. "Why, so can I, and so can any man." "But *will they come* when you do call for them?" rejoins Hotspur. As Christians, we may be extremely doubtful as to the propriety of curiosity in this connexion. As scientific enquirers, we must admit remarkable evidence as to communication, but need not admit that this is evidence for more than telepathic communication at second remove. (The idea, the factual information, may be available in the mind of a third person and revealed to a second by a first, both of the latter being hitherto unaware of the item concerned.)

As judges of quality, we must also admit that the literacy, the spiritual and artistic quality, of *all* communications hitherto made available is profoundly disappointing to anyone who had looked for matter of importance. If it is indeed the poets who communicate with mediums the next world would appear to have a most unfortunate effect upon their poetic powers.

But the story of Endor, however we come to interpret the details, is a reminder that no one can escape the consequence of his actions by enlisting supernatural help. If and in so far as such help can genuinely claim either insight into reality or perception of the hidden springs of the human personality, it can only endorse the honest judgement of the upright mind. More often, perhaps, it offers the soul a flattering unction which will only conceal reality for the moment and still further delay courageous decision.

2 SAMUEL 11 and 12. 1–24

45

FROM CUCKOLDRY TO MURDER

THIS IS ONE OF THE GREAT stories of mankind, and must be read as a whole. Like so many other dramas of the Old Testament, its reading is too long for a "lesson" in church, and so it is seldom heard or considered in full. Yet almost every word is significant.

It begins in the springtime, when hill tracks become fit for campaigning. The army is away at the front, and the king stays at home in Jerusalem. One day, getting up from his siesta, and taking an evening stroll on the palace roof — in the agreeable hour of "sundowners" and pink gin — he sees, looking out over the roofs of the city, a girl having a bath. Enquiry shows that she is the wife of a foreigner away serving in the army. David therefore seduces her — but later learns she is expecting a baby. Verse 5 sums up tersely a situation that has occurred millions of times in the world's history — a situation of catastrophic potentiality. David meets his perilous responsibility immediately, by seeing that Uriah is sent back home on a military mission, with the idea that he may sleep with his wife and unconsciously accept paternity of the child she is expecting. And here the most tragic part of the whole unhappy story begins. All through the tale it is Uriah's *good* qualities which David, that percipient psychologist, shamelessly manipulates, or which otherwise contribute to their owner's death.

So Uriah refuses to accept privileges and comforts he cannot share with his fellow-combatants still in the field. David in desperation exploits the possibilities of royal hospitality — and a properly courteous acceptance of it — by getting him drunk in the hope that his self-control will be broken down. Still no good. Uriah sleeps it off in the guard-room. Now for political murder. David arranges that the bravery of Uriah shall lead to his death. Not only shall he be encouraged to lead a desperate assault, but he is to be deserted in the breach — along, incidentally, with other fighting men who were unlucky enough to be caught up in the royal intrigue.

Cynical messages of *"double entendre"* pass between king and C-and-C. Uriah duly dies, and, after a respectable interval, his wife remarries.

So far, a not-unknown situation. The boss, the man of power, seducing a junior's wife, frightened of the consequences, and led, step-by-step, into murder. Theodore Dreiser's compelling book, *An American Tragedy* shows a development not dissimilar — only, as it were, in reverse. Here it is the girl who dies, so that the seducer's career may not suffer.

But now for a new element. Nathan, a man as intelligent as David and of total integrity, confronts the king with a situation which compels him to give his official judgement before he is aware that it is his own case of which he is judge : he condemns himself — and thereby is confronted with the crime he has committed, the guilt he must accept. However we interpret the baby's death that follows, David and Nathan both regard it as part of his punishment — and David takes that with dignity — even if his attitude to mourning does rather suggest that he had hoped to win God round rather than to admit his own sin! And in due course these two remarkable people, David and Bathsheba, produce another child, who will inherit all and more than all their intelligence, all and more than all their sexual susceptibility, but perhaps rather less of their human tenderness.

This is a story whose application there is no need to stress — unless it is to warn us of that corruption of all moral values which supposes that "Love" is at once the justification of any form of disloyalty and dishonesty and that no ties, personal or official, can possibly be allowed to stand in its way.

2 SAMUEL 18. 9–33

46

MY SON, MY SON

EVERY SON WHO ADMIRES HIS father — and most do, at least in their earliest years — is confronted by two possibilities. Either he must compete with his father and excel him at his own game, or else he must play quite a different game, which he will make his own. To follow in his father's footsteps, but to go neither so far nor so fast, is to strain their relationship from both ends. The son is frustrated, feeling himself only a pale copy rather than a bold original : the father is disappointed, and finds it almost impossible not to make his disappointment obvious.

Absalom, son of David, was born to him of "Maacah,

daughter of Talmir, King of Geshur". We know nothing about her, though we know a good deal about her son. For one thing, he was a man of long-term patience. He waited two years, for instance, to revenge himself upon his elder brother (and, incidentally, to get rid of the direct heir to the throne): the story of this is in 2 Samuel 13. For another, he was a man of exceptional distinction of appearance — perhaps, also, of vanity, and certainly of charm. The whole story of his insinuation of himself back into favour, first, with his indignant father, and second, with the people, deserves reading (chapters 14 and 15). His technique was simple. First, he made friends with the chief-of-staff, and secured his collaboration. Then he "stole the hearts of the men of Israel" by indicating how generous a monarch he would himself make. Third, he declared open rebellion, and suborned Ahithophel, his father's own minister of state. It is now that David shows his own greatness — and indeed his own personality.

For his nearer friends, including the Foreign Legion recruited from the Philistines, stand by him, as do the clergy. In no time (see chapter 15), a fifth column is planted in Absalom's own camp.

Meantime (see chapter 16) the conflict is made absolute when Absalom deliberately violates his father's harem, thus not only claiming the privileges of monarchy but also asserting the end of any family tie. Peaceful solution is deliberately made impossible.

Chapter 17 describes the alternative plan offered him. The oily and faithless Ahithophel urges that a flying column pursue after David, harrying him into the ground, whilst Absalom tightens his hold on the country, but keeps in hand his main army. Hushai, David's secret ally, however, persuades Absalom to hazard his own life — and his entire striking force — in a pitched battle in the forests on the east side of Jordan. This was a mistake: one equally bad was to get rid of the hard-bitten old soldier, Joab, and appoint his cousin Amasa as commander-in-chief. The battle went in favour of David, and Absalom was killed. In the last part of chapter 18 there is reference to the ancient habit of rewarding the bearer of good tidings and punish-

97

ing, even with death, the bearer of bad. It was, therefore, very important to assess just how a given message was likely to be received and to send an expendable man with a doubtful one (as in this case) rather than to hazard the life of a friend.

It is an unhappy story, this, of a young man of immense ability but overwhelming ambition. He had many of his father's qualities — and knew it. But he lacked David's immense generosity of temperament — and he found himself in the position of all mutineers (even of such honourable men as Fletcher Christian of the *Bounty*). Loyal men become enemies : one's own supporters include those whose motives are self-seeking as well as those who are for justice. It is hard to distinguish between the two. It is hard to find honest counsellors and men of genuine reliability. It is easier to destroy the evil in an external authority (which is the cause of honourable rebellion) than to eliminate it from one's own supporters.

2 SAMUEL 23. 8–22

47

BRAVER THAN THE LION

CULTURES AND CIVILISATIONS have differed a great deal in their judgement as to good and evil, but there never was a nation or a man that did not admire courage. David, himself a farmer, a musician, a bandit, and a king, had a very proper respect for anyone who showed qualities appropriate to each of these occupations, from common-sense at one end of the scale to magnanimity at the other. But of all qualities he loved courage the most, and so distributed positions in his kingdom to men in accordance with the degree to which they showed it. How interesting our own government would be if its cabinets were appointed on the same principle !

But what, precisely, *is* courage? The answers are manifold. The passage before us contains at least four of them. First, courage consists — in part at least — of the power of leadership and of inspiring strength in others by one's own example. A really brave man makes others brave. Two of the four officers listed in this passage proved their courage by standing fast when others ran for it — and the strength of their example recalled the waverers and won the day. In this sense, courage is a faith in others, a loyalty to the man below even greater than that to the man above — the quality seen to perfection in Abraham Lincoln.

Second, courage involves an element of self-sacrifice for others. Very many of the accepted heroics of courage have been performed by men (or women) in saving other people, rather than in doing something on their own. It may be the wife sucking poison from the husband's wound, the comrade going out under fire to fetch in an injured comrade, the miner battling through rockfalls and gas to look for his mates. Three friends of David, hearing him speak with homesickness of the cool spring in his own village of Bethlehem, go at the risk of their lives to fetch him a draught of it. He honours them — and himself — by offering it to God, with the implication that he himself was unworthy of such courage and such devotion. When love is involved men do not count the cost, any more than Mary considered the value of the oil of spikenard which she poured over Jesus' feet. There is a generosity of love which often expresses itself in the language of courage, like the mother bird or rabbit which will defy the snake for its babies' sake.

Third, there is a total refusal to consider "the lore of nicely-calculated less and more". Are there eight hundred of the enemy? or three hundred? or just "a troop"? Have you weapons in your hand? or only a cudgel? no matter. In the words of a great Frenchman — "I am your king. You are Frenchmen. Yonder is the foe. Let us attack him."

The courageous man resembles that tiny Athenian army at Marathon, which, seeing the vast Persian army overspreading the plain, advanced upon it at the double — and advanced to victory. Courage is sometimes its own form of arithmetic — unlike the soldier who said "I feel like ten men. Nine are dead and one sick."

Fourth, courage is not afraid of the unknown. Consider the case of Benaiah, the son of Jehoiada, in verse 20. It is a time of snow, when men literally have "cold feet". He finds the lion that has been destroying stock — maybe human lives too — trapped in a pitfall, or tumbled, perhaps, into a granary dug out for corn. Common-sense said "fetch help" — "shoot from a distance" — but down into the pit he leaps and engages the lion, man-to-beast, with space only to fight. It seems a pity "Benaiah" has never taken on popularity as a Christian name. Could there be any finer namesake than this, the captain of David's guard and so clearly his most trusted friend?

Of course, there are many kinds of courage not illustrated here. There is moral courage in all its many forms — not least in the willingness to "be different", and the faith which can "dare to be a Daniel, dare to stand alone". We shall find, however, plenty of examples of these other forms of courage elsewhere in the Bible. This particular passage reminds us that physical courage has a glory of its own and that the greatest of Hebrew kings honoured it accordingly. Indeed, did not a later "Son of David" show this same physical courage in accepting and enduring torment and death without flinching?

1 KINGS 12. 1–16

48

"TO YOUR TENTS, O ISRAEL"

SOLOMON LEFT TO HIS SON A wealthy and important kingdom — almost a small empire, if one thinks of its trade-routes and outpost ports. But he did not leave to him that wisdom which has made his father's name a byword ever since.

Rehoboam, like many a young man inheriting a family business (whether in the line of kingship or conventional commerce) had his own ideas. He had his own cronies, too, the contemporaries who had been at school with him. So soon as he ascended the throne, he had to receive a deputation — as it might be, a delegation of shop stewards — headed by Jeroboam.

This last was a young man, the son of a widow, who as a result had had to make his own way in the world and had proved himself capable and very hard working. He had been in trouble as a suspected revolutionary, and had only returned to the country when the king's death seemed to make return safe.

The deputation asked for some relaxation of working conditions. Would the new boss, they wanted to know, be prepared to meet their demands? Sensibly, he asks for time and calls in his top management for consultation.

They are all for conciliation. Meet the men half-way, they say, and you'll have them with you for the future. But then he goes to his cronies. "Don't be a fool," they say, "show 'em who's master. Begin as you mean to go on." So he does as weak men so often do; he tries to put up an impressive façade. He blusters. "If my father was tough," he says, "I'll be tougher still. Get back to work — and to harder work than ever."

At this, Jeroboam blows the whistle and calls the factory out. That's to say, the greater part of the factory. Ten of the twelve tribes, all of them except Judah and Benjamin (which means, geographically, all the north and central districts of Israel) break away from the rest and put themselves under the rule of Jeroboam as their elected king. But Jerusalem, the holy city, remains in the Southern kingdom, which will be known as Judah whilst the North will be called Israel. So the Northerners will have to find a capital city — which they do in Samaria — and a place for worship, which they do in the ancient sanctuary of Beth-el.

For the next centuries these two kingdoms will be separated, either living on terms of uneasy truce or engaged in open war until Samaria is captured and destroyed by invaders — and less than forty years later, Jerusalem shares the same fate. The bluster of a weak man can be more disastrous than the toughness of a strong one. Nothing is so dangerous as a bluff that is called. The story of Rehoboam might well be compulsory reading for all students of business administration.

49

ALARM AND DESPONDENCY

DEPRESSION IS NOT A MODERN discovery. In all ages all sorts of people have had times when they felt either that the world was all wrong — frustration — or else that they were all wrong themselves — failure. The first feeling may have in it a genuine measure of honest compassion, the second one of true humility. But both these motives are counterbalanced by elements of pride (why can't *I* do more about it?), weariness (I've tried and tried, and it's no good) and even an active death-wish (oh, to hell with it all).

Depression very often accompanies over-work, and by its very nature is a part of over-worry. So it is not much wonder that the lonely giant, Elijah, should suffer from a severe attack. Apart from everything else, he is a proscribed man, on the run for his life, and most of his friends have been murdered.

And the treatment he gets is very much the treatment a good doctor might have recommended today. First of all, immediate rest and sleep. Then, an unexciting but digestible and sustaining diet. And after it, exercise and travel. This puts him into a state when he is capable of sensible thought and indeed of deep spiritual experience. The story of that experience is as revealing as the nature of the treatment he has already received. He begins, as we are all apt to do, by pouring out his own problems and difficulties. "I've done everything I could . . . but they're all against me, everyone of them . . . there's no one on my side . . . they're out to get me too."

And he gets his answer. First, a revelation of tremendous irresistible power — power in earthquake, wind, and fire. But though this power is dependent upon God, though it obeys his will, yet it is not the expression of his nature. Elijah has thought in terms of power-politics, has looked for a revelation of God overthrowing his enemies by superior strength. But this is not the divine way. The sound and the fury pass away, and then in the deep silence that falls, a still small voice speaks. It is a voice that countless millions have heard, a voice that speaks from and in the deepest part of each one of us. And it asks him the question that conscience so often asks the rest of us: "What are you doing here?" — with the emphasis varying from the first word to the last — "What-are-you-doing-here?" Elijah replies — as, again, we are all apt to do — with a recital of his problems and difficulties, building up to a climax of self-pity.

He finds no sympathy at all. On the contrary, he is literally sent about his business. "Go straight back: anoint two new kings — and your own successor" — with the pointed addition that there are still seven thousand people beside himself who are undergoing the same trials and have shown no less fortitude. Nor need we imagine that his king-making mission was an agreeable one, or likely to be popular with the despotic kings who were at that moment in power. He is not only sent back into the hornet's nest — into two hornets' nests: but he also has instructions to stir them both up with a stick. But he goes — and perhaps the problem of how the job was to be done overcame his depression — just as the company of Elisha must certainly have cured his loneliness.

This is not only a most moving account of despair and how to treat it: it is also a very vivid picture of how God deals with a human soul in need and gives it precisely what is most helpful for it in its particular situation. Self-pity is a disease which attacks us all: no remedies could be more sensible or more effective than those prescribed for Elijah.

I KINGS 21. 1–20

50

TOM TIDDLER'S GROUND

AHAB MAY WELL HAVE BEEN ONE of the worst kings of Israel, but he was certainly one of the most interesting. His relationship with the prophet Elijah is a little like that of King Henry to Thomas à Becket. Each was attracted by the other, each respected the other — yet each felt compelled to fight against the other to the death.

His wife was a foreigner, a woman clearly of great fascination as well as great force of character — and entirely without moral scruple. Brought up in the tradition of absolute power, she could see no objection to its use so that when her husband wants to buy a small vineyard to round off the palace gardens she is amazed at his Jewish respect for law and tradition. She sees that downright expropriation — the way which would have been pursued today — will cause trouble. How much easier to exploit religious prejudice and make the *people* the murderers of Naboth! Then, if there is any subsequent trouble, the mob can be blamed — or, if need be, the two purchased witnesses sacrificed to the claims of justice.

Everything goes according to plan, but the plan comes to pieces when the infuriating prophet turns up to challenge the king's right to his new property. Turns up, like the conscience he was — a conscience which the king himself recognises. At the end of this chapter, indeed, it is even suggested that the king reformed his ways — though this may have been the explanation offered by the writer for the fact that retribution did not strike, as had been expected, until the next monarch's reign.

Ahab, then, is a kind of Macbeth. A man not totally bad, but of uncontrolled desires and temper. He would not deliberately kill to satisfy his immediate wish — but his wife would, and he would not be inclined to ask too many questions about it afterwards.

What about Naboth? We can think of him as an obstinate man offered very reasonable compensation, but stubborn in his refusal to budge — the sort of man whose property is the very last to be acquired when a new housing site is planned.

Or we can think of him as a man of the highest moral integrity, a smallholder who has inherited the family farm and means to pass it on to his children, after giving his life to its improvement. In that case his refusal is heroic. How much easier and safer to have fallen in with the royal wish, to have accepted the alternative accommodation offered or the "golden handshake". How hard to hold out, knowing that this must mean the beginning of an endless persecution, of summonses for this and that, of market consignments unaccountably gone astray and documents missing. But if he is to keep faith with the family tradition he can do no other. Such men were the Covenanters and the Pilgrim Fathers, dour men, infuriating in their obstinacy, yet rocklike in their strength. They can be broken, but they will not bend.

The really contemptible people in this story are the "elders and nobles", the comfortable courtiers and prosperous citizens who knew the whole charge was trumped-up, but were willing to oblige the queen by selling their honour. Ahab has a certain integrity, even a royalty, about him. Jezebel has such dignity as an absorbing, passionate love may give. Naboth is a man no one can fail to respect — Elijah, like John the Baptist, towers over them all. But at the bottom come the creepers and fawners, the people who won't criticise the boss even when they know his methods are crooked. It is the condemnation of absolute power that it encourages such creatures, and that their very presence drives away the men like Elijah whose integrity is necessary to it. It is hard for the very rich girl to find a good husband — since good men are the most unwilling to appear fortune-hunters. It is hard for the very rich young man to discover friends who are neither attracted nor put off by his opulence, but can like him for himself alone.

2 KINGS 2. 1–18

51

ASCENT TO HEAVEN

THERE ARE TWO GREAT MEN WHO typify to us, as to their own nation and perhaps indeed to God (Mark 9, verse 4), the best of the Old Testament. Neither of them is supposed to have met a normal end. Moses, denied the privilege of entering the promised land, died in the foreign territory of Moab, and found an unknown grave (Deuteronomy 23, verse 6). He represented in his person the whole concept of organised religion, moral law and priesthood, yet combined with his authority a deep sense of compassion and a touching humility. The other great man, Elijah, symbolised prophecy — personal holiness, personal commitment and individual responsibility, the direct contact of divinity with chosen persons, the powers that resulted from it. He was God's messenger, as Moses was God's regent. Of course the two functions are complementary and must occasionally overlap. For example, the prophet is concerned with social righteousness as much as is the lawgiver. Yet perhaps the prophet's special duty is to bring home to the *individual,* king or widow woman, what the general moral imperative means for their own particular case. It is, a little unexpectedly, the grim prophet rather than the law-giver who is to return to earth as the forerunner of the promised Messiah.

His death, then, since he is to be so honoured, must be unusual. Perhaps, indeed, he ought not to die at all, but to share that destiny which one verbal interpretation had allowed to the patriarch Enoch (see Genesis 5, verse 24): that of direct assumption in the body from earth to heaven? Perhaps, if he is to return to earth as harbinger of the kingdom, he ought to be alive in the body to announce the coming of it?

Now, as Christians, we are not compelled to accept the literal truth of this story, and to suppose that Christ's ascension was anticipated by Elijah. We may remember how many great and holy men, of various religions, have disappeared into a kind of permanent retreat before the end of their mortal life. We may remember how subsequent admirers have developed this withdrawal into the idea of direct assumption into another world (with which they so clearly were already familiar).

But it is difficult to put any such interpretation on the story of Elijah's ascent. First, because some such idea was evidently in the mind of his friends (verses 16 to 18 of this chapter). Second, because Elijah himself did everything possible to avoid having any witness of what happened — but without success (verses 1 to 6). He really does try hard to shake off the persistent Elisha and covers a lot of country in doing it and in making a round of farewell visits. Third, most significant, when Elisha asks for a special gift of grace, of that perception of the divine will which had been Elijah's strength, he is told that it is not in the prophet's power to give. But the sign that God has indeed bestowed it would be his own ability to perceive the link between God and man expressed in Elijah's journey home. If Elisha can "see" this moment of spiritual truth, then he is indeed already a "seer".

It is possible, of course, to explain (or explain away) many of the details. Elisha's description of his predecessor as the strength of the nation — "its chariot and horsemen" — could, if overheard, presuppose an actual heavenly chariot: it could be that the cloak from the dead Elijah symbolised the transfer of his authority as the coronation crown represents kingly authority; that Elijah chose to die somewhere in the solitariness beyond Jordan and sent his follower back in his name to carry on his work, or that Elisha's reason for trying to prevent a search was his knowledge that Elijah was determined to be alone with his God in death.

But we are certainly on common ground, however we interpret or explain the details, if we find in this story recognition of the fact that to every great man (indeed, to little ones as well) there comes a moment for laying aside power and authority, and for seeing that somebody else ought to take on his job. Elijah's greatness consists not least in his immediate acceptance of this, and his perfect readiness to surrender his position to another. This is the man whom God has designated as his successor? Then God alone can give the ability to carry out the duties to be undertaken: all that Elijah does is first to test the other's strength and determination, and then to hand over the task to him, without extensive farewell and without effort to impose a future plan. His own work is done, he returns to his father's house. *"Le roi est mort: vive le roi."* Into thy hands, O Lord . . .

52

MIND YOUR MANNERS

THIS IS A DEPLORABLE STORY.
Nasty little boys (Revised Standard Version) shout at an elderly
parson, who loses his temper and shouts back — with the result,
apparently, that they all suffer a violent death.

> *Forty-two children lay dead on the sward*
> *Forty-two children, or possibly more,*
> *For the bears were too busy the sum to record*
> *And the prophet didn't stay to attend to the score.*

The facts of the story, presumably, are essentially as follows.
Rude children — or possibly adolescents — jeered at Elisha, on
the grounds of physical appearance (as they might have mocked
at a cripple). He rebuked them, and a little while after they
were attacked by two bears and a number died. (It is tempting
to suppose they were teasing the bears or throwing stones at their
cubs.) People associated the two incidents and regarded one as
the cause of the other, whereas they were simply associated in
time. But, whilst we can be sure that the God who called little
children to him most certainly does not massacre them on the
ground of a moment's rudeness or of passing bad temper on the
part of one of his servants, there is meaning in the story.

Are children really "irresponsible" whatever they do? We
know, from experience, just what they can do out of "mischief".
They can derail a train with loss of life, stab one another, destroy
the laboriously planted flowers of a park, wreck the interior of
a church — and, perhaps much worse, they can, by bullying,
corrupt and frighten one another to permanent effect. Are all
these things unimportant just because the doers of them are not
of mature age? Is there not a risk that we can corporately spoil
children by our attitude to their every doing, just as we can
individually spoil them within the family circle? We can, that
is to say, undervalue the crime out of pity for the criminal.

Now this does *not* mean, as an alternative, that we are to

execute little children for theft or clap them into prison for breaking windows. But it does mean that we ought to think out much more carefully and responsibly how we can detect — and cure — in embryo stages the attitudes which will later develop into real evil. Mere softness is a sort of appeasement, which children are quite realist enough to exploit.

Here is a case in point. Sneering at the other people's physical shortcomings is a detestable sort of behaviour, which can develop into persecution. What had the parents of the children done about it? — had they thought it "cute" and encouraged the children in what they thought an amusing game? or perhaps, encouraged them to despise and attack strangers?

In this case, the same children who had been playing their familiar game, came to a bloody end. Whose fault was it? And how does it affect us today? Are we surprised and unhappy if the children we teach to be competitive and self-centred come to despise weakness instead of helping it? If those whom we have plied with expensive possessions instead of understanding and companionship came to believe that love too is to be bought and sold? If those who have seen no evidence in our lives of concern with anything beyond our own wishes themselves become cynical and contemptuous?

The brash and offensive child, the spoiled brat and the pampered adolescent, these are not harmless young things who will one day "grow out of it"; they are the adults of the future — and we are responsible for forming them to this pattern.

2 KINGS 4. 8–37

53

GREATNESS OF HEART

LATIN WRITERS SPOKE WITH AD-miration of a quality they called "magnanimity" — greatness of mind and heart. It was a quality difficult to describe but easy to recognise; it had in it the simplicity of the pure in heart, the integrity of the upright, the generosity of the unselfish.

This particular story in front of us is a picture of how "magnanimity" can be encountered in everyday life. There is a greatness and dignity about the lady of Shunem which is most moving — a greatness which echoes that of her friend the prophet Elisha.

The story begins in a familiar setting. The lady of the manor entertains the visiting preacher. They take to each other, and seeing how often he passes through their town, she arranges for a guest chamber to be at his disposal. It is "on the wall" — accessible from outside: he has, as it were, a latch-key. Elisha is very grateful, and is anxious to show his gratitude. Can he perhaps commend her at court (where he is highly respected, a sort of archiepiscopal figure)? She makes a magnificent reply. *This*, she says, is where she belongs, here at home, amongst her neighbours and friends.

So Elisha talks the matter over with his trusted servant, Gehazi, and learns that above all else — she longs for a child. In due course, her son is born.

Then there follows an incident of infinite pathos. The child goes harvesting with his father, playing the man among men. But the sun is too much for him; he is carried home prostrate with heat-stroke, to die on his mother's knee.

And now, note her faith and determination. She calls for transport, and makes off as fast as it is possible to travel. No one can help except the man of God, nor will she give a message to any other. He respects her grief, and sends Gehazi carrying his master's staff (a badge of delegated authority, like the king's signet ring in later history) with strict orders to stop on the road for nothing. But the mother is not content with any delegated authority: she insists that Elisha come himself, and waits until he does. She was right: the staff produced no result. This is a situation where not only must the prophet himself intervene, but he must work hard if he is to succeed.

This need for effort gives meaning to what follows, an incident paralleled in our own "kiss of life" technique for dealing with the apparently drowned. There is no instantaneous result. Elisha has first to pray, then get to work at the healing. Next he must gather together all his strength, and return to work at it again. And now the child comes back into the world he had left, back either from a coma or from death itself.

There is about the whole story a strange anticipation of the healing ministry of Christ himself. There is the gracious courtesy of exchanged gifts at the beginning, the immediate certainty on the part of the Shunammite that there is a power in this man on which she can depend, her justified refusal to deal with any underling, her determination that she will not take "no" for an answer. Here greatness meets greatness, and each respects and indeed loves the other's high quality.

2 KINGS 5. 1–19

54

HOME TALENT

THIS STORY, LIKE THE LAST, IS A tale of "magnanimity" — and, as in the last instance, it is found in two people — and two people of very different background. One is a distinguished soldier and the other a captive child. The soldier, Naaman, has served his country of Syria well, but in the course of his campaigning has contracted the hideous disease of leprosy. It must have been in its earliest stages as he is still living at home, respected, even loved, as well as pitied by his household. In this household is a little Jewish girl, captured by a raiding band as they sacked and burned her native village.

The child has not forgotten her home, though she has settled down cheerfully to do her best in her strange new life. Like the others, she pities her master and says confidently that her own Jewish prophet would be just the man to cure him. This tale is carried to Naaman himself. Desperate, he will try anything, and his friend the king will surely help. As one king to another, he will write to the King of Israel. As a great king to a small one, his message reads "kindly oblige by return, or else . . ."

The King of Israel is quick enough to see the implication —

but luckily Elisha, the prophet in question, hears of the royal anxiety. "Send him on to me," he says, and very willingly the king does so. In due course a great cavalcade draws up at the door of the little house and a messenger demands to speak with the prophet.

Elisha is not impressed. A young man comes to the door, gives a message and goes back into the house again — and Naaman is furious. "To come all this way and be told to paddle in a filthy little stream," he says, "no proper consultation — no full-scale healing-service".

And now the real affection of his servants is evident. They address him with love as well as respect. "Nothing would be too *much* to do in the hope of getting well," they say; "are you too proud to do a small thing?"

And, of course, it works. Afterwards, overjoyed, Naaman will pay any price, do anything, to show his gratitude. But no, the prophet wants none of it. And then Naaman again shows his real "magnanimity". He sees that the prophet has been trying to show him that this is God's doing, not man's, and that the only thing he can give to God in recognition is himself. But this is a God of the neighbourhood, a God who belongs hereabouts. How do you worship him outside his own territory? Why, easy, take a bit of it with you. Then you can always find him at home. But stop, what about those state occasions when Syria's own God has to be worshipped — full-dress parades, royal attendance, court ceremonial? Will it be cheating if he attends, or will it be all right? "Go in peace," says the prophet.

Now before we smile at the "superstition" of Naaman, we had better think of our own attitude towards Holy Things. A Christian "relic" is simply an object closely and personally associated with a saint, and believed to retain something of that holiness thereafter. Is our veneration of relics so very different from carrying home two mules' burden of soil? And what about our own consecrating of an altar-slab to be a sort of portable church so that whenever it is put down, the Eucharist may properly be celebrated?

All this seems to be linked with that deep traditional conviction that places and objects may carry with them what primitive man calls "mana", an indwelling power. It is this "mana" which makes objects of "fetish" or "totem" dangerous, so that to touch them improperly is to release a killing power (of the story of Uzzah and the Ark: 2 Samuel 6, verses 6 to 11).

But is this belief necessarily "unscientific"? For thousands of years it would have seemed ludicrous to say that a piece of copper wire could be turned into a lethal weapon because it was connected with a machine fifty miles away. Electric conductivity we accept as a fact: is it possible there is some sort of spiritual conductivity, by which a spiritual power, for good or ill, is released in and through places and things? Is this a possible explanation of "haunting"?

This is a story of greatness of heart. Greatness of heart in a little girl who could feel compassion for the people who had made her prisoner: greatness of heart in servants who dared to defy a powerful master for his good: greatness of heart in a man who gave to God in thanksgiving the one thing that cannot be bought — himself.

2 KINGS 6. 1–23

55

HOW TO DEAL WITH AN ENEMY

WE ARE ACCUSTOMED TO THINK-ing of the Old Testament as steeped in violence. Populations are exterminated, cities sacked, individuals executed. Any outbreak of sin is treated by the methods we employ in dealing with an outbreak of foot-and-mouth disease — the wholesale slaughter of all who may possibly have been infected. Yet this same Old Testament has moments in which the reader's eyes are opened to the real nature of God and his will for man. These moments are usually to be found in the writings of the prophets, and reach their climax in the last chapter of Isaiah. But they are also recorded in the stories of individual lives, and even in the chapters of national history. The particular incident before us

H

deserves to be read both for its own sake and for all that it implies as to our own contemporary social attitudes.

But before the main theme, there comes a valuable preface. Elisha and the young men who attended him — pupils, disciples, admirers, seminarists, and what-have-you — are building a log-cabin, felling trees in the dense forests of Jordan-side. One loses his axe-head (very precious indeed in an age when all metals, bronze and iron both, were rare and expensive).

We can, if we like, rationalise the story by supposing that Elisha simply told him to stop panicking and show him just where the axe-head fell into the water. That he then threw in a stone and suggested that diving in that area would find the hatchet. Or else we can be quite literalist, and can draw our-selves a charming picture of the iron swimming up from the river bottom and attaching itself to the wooden handle thrown in after it, as a life-belt to a drowning man. But in either case, let us be concerned with the attitude of the young man, whose main grief it was that he had lost something borrowed. Perhaps there are two sorts of person, those who, like this youth, worry more over how they treat a borrowed suit, or car, or book, or country cottage, and those who worry *less*. Even those people, who are careful with a personal loan, can be irresponsible when what they are using is a piece of public property, a library book, or the firm's car; those of us who would respect the tidi-ness of a friend's garden are quite capable of leaving our litter on a National Trust beauty spot.

But after this preface, we come to the main adventure. The neighbour-state, Syria, is conducting one of its regular frontier wars with the Northern Kingdom of Israel.

There appears to be a serious breakdown in military security, and the King of Syria sets afoot an enquiry into its reason. He is told that it is not so much a matter of treachery within as of supernatural espionage. Israel is getting advance information of all his plans before they are even on paper. Now this is intoler-able, and he decides on rapid action. A strong striking force is ordered to arrest the prophet immediately, and, after a night march, is moved into a position surrounding the little town where he is staying. Elisha's attendant, taking an early walk, discovers what has happened and panics. He is only comforted when it is made clear to him that the prophet does not rely on human defences.

Now comes the hub of the story. Notice how Elisha is not prepared to escape himself, leaving the town to be destroyed. Whether or not the Syrians are *literally* blinded, he certainly persuades them (a) that he is himself not Elisha but (b) that he will show them where Elisha is to be found. He then leads them into the cantonments of his own capital city, where the excited king, stammering with excitement, proposes to wipe out the invaders. But NO, says Elisha, spare their lives, feed them well — and send them home.

Prisoners, he says, are *not* to be massacred, whether they are taken after combat or not. They are to be treated as fellow-beings, and properly looked after.

This all happened three thousand years ago. There are few signs that we have learned the lesson. Yet in verse 23 the moral is drawn, clear enough. Elisha's generosity was more effective than any military action. By sparing the prisoners and sending them home to tell of it, he made a fair and lasting peace.

2 KINGS 9. 1–24

56

DANGEROUS DRIVING

ONE OF THE PROBLEMS OF EVERY dictator is that of selecting his military officers. If they are capable, they are likely to be ambitious — and so possible claimants to the dictator's throne. If they are *not* capable, then they will be no defence against attack from other quarters. The dictator's only hope of stability is either to pick a general who is both able and loyal (difficult to find), or one who is capable, indeed, but also self-indulgent and lazy. And all the time he must be very wary about the emergence of likely rivals to himself from amongst those who control his military resources.

The story before us is the story of a military coup of this kind. Elisha, both prophet and politician, has selected a young but capable and hard-hitting colonel as the future monarch of Israel. He knows his man, and the kind of message that will bring an immediate response — a message calling for instant and violent action. Jehu pauses only to sound out his comrades, and with their enthusiastic support, strikes hard and quickly.

All that follows has been repeated a thousand times since. The march on the royal city — the pickets riding out in apprehension and instantly enlisted — even the king's personal action in the effort to win back his officer's loyalty.

But there is one phrase that has made this story memorable — verse 20 — the furious driving of Jehu. In that single sentence is all the interpretation of character revealed in a man's attitudes and actions.

It is, of course, still true. We can diagnose a great deal about people's disposition from the way they drive. First of all, there are the "Pharisees" of the road. These are the elderly people in elderly cars who drive in the very middle of the highway rather slower than the speed-limit allows, and bitterly resent being passed by others. They are the cause of innumerable minor accidents — indignant as they would be at the suggestion — because of the frustration they cause to other drivers. Of course people have a right to drive slowly, but this right involves a responsibility for helping faster vehicles — as one often finds with, say, tractor drivers — and is not an absolute claim in itself. Such people are often revealed as self-righteous, limited in sympathy, lacking in imagination.

The "Publicans" of the road are much more obvious. They are the people who not only take risks, but inflict them on other people. Now this does not necessarily go with fast driving. There are drivers, roads, and cars (in that order), for whom and for which high speed is perfectly safe. But in each of these cases the number of such is considerably less than is normally supposed. Our trouble is that we tend to drive competitively rather than co-operatively. We feel better men, stronger, braver men, when we pass other people, or when we manage to outstrip a larger or newer car than our own.

And this competitive attitude leads to a refusal to give way, whether it be a matter of allowing a car out of a side-street to enter a traffic flow (when it would make only twenty feet of difference to ourselves to allow him in!), or of permitting someone who has got into the wrong stream to come across into the right one.

Because we won't give way, we compel other drivers, if they're to get along at all, to do it by getting tough and just pushing their way into the traffic-stream — and then we feel resentful.

Quite a high proportion of the digestive and other upsets produced by frustration must be encouraged by our driving manners — and people who behave with courtesy and charm on their two feet become offensive boors on four wheels.

Jehu, that furious driver, revealed himself as bloodthirsty and self-willed; he managed to murder, in his zeal for the Lord, a remarkable number of his fellow-children of God. As a Christian nation, we too manage to murder upon the roads quite a number of our brothers and sisters in Christ annually. Does our driving, like his, reveal our own disposition?

2 KINGS 17. 1–6 and 24–28

57

THE LIONS OF SAMARIA

WHY DID THE JEWS HATE THE Samaritans so bitterly? Like most feuds this one had become an emotional tradition rather than a national attitude. It went back six hundred years, to the time when the one people had split up into two nations — the nation of Israel, having its capital at Samaria, and the nation of Judah, with its capital city, Jerusalem.

The two fought out a bitter series of border-wars, fierce as those of, say, England and Scotland; and like England and Scotland, they had their times of peace, and also their common enemies. It was one of the latter, Assyria, which finally overran Israel in 722 B.C.

Now, when a city and nation were defeated, there were three possible courses open to the victor. He could make them into "tributaries" levying demands in cash and menpower, but allowing a considerable degree of self-government (except in foreign affairs): he could utterly destroy the victim state, carrying its women into slavery and exterminating its men; or he could transport the majority of the population to new homes elsewhere in his dominions, recolonising the city-state with settlers shifted from elsewhere (rather as in schemes of slum-clearance).

It was this, a not unmerciful policy, which Shalmaneser, Emperor of Assyria, meted out to Samaria. And it was very successful, so much so that the people of Israel settled down in their new homes, lost their identity, and became known to speculative history ever since as "The Ten Lost Tribes".

The new colonists in Samaria found themselves in trouble. They were bothered by swarms — technically, "Prides" — of lions. (At this time lions ranged over most of the Middle East, as is clear from both sculptural and scriptural evidence.) It immediately occurred to them that this was due to the anger of the local deity, whose ways they had not learned to understand. Accordingly, they wrote home for immediate action, and a Jewish priest was sent to them. He re-established the Jewish faith, but it was, not unnaturally perhaps, conflated with that of all the national gods whom the settlers had brought with them, reminders of their lost homelands and the culture of their ancestors (just exactly as, forty years later, the people of Jerusalem would take *their* worship to Babylon!). It was this "contaminated" Judaism which was the religion of the Samaritans in Gospel times, and it was the contamination, the surrender to the Gentile world, which aroused the fury of the orthodox Jewry.

Now the Samaritans cannot claim very lofty motives for their change of faith. At the best, theirs was the attitude of the Englishman in Africa who suspects there may be "something in" ju-ju or devil-worship and prefers not to put it to the test. At the worst, it was that of the man who will change his faith if it pays, abandoning an earlier one which proves locally unpopular, and selecting another which offers inducements. But let us be fair to them. Gods, as far as they were concerned, were strictly local (see 1 Kings 20, verse 23 for a parallel view). They were the deities who lived in a particular spring or wood; who, by extension, were to be found at home in a special temple, or keeping company with a favoured nation. When entering their territory, one naturally made polite acknowledgement. But to the Jews, this attitude was intolerable — and we must sympathise with them. God, they said, is the Lord of the whole earth, and holds all the nations in his hand. To turn him into a godling with a rustic accent is monstrous.

The trouble was that though their concept of God was extraterritorial and international, their concept of themselves was not. He was to be *their* God, and to limit his favours strictly to them.

This was what galled them about the Samaritans — as the same element (call it "contamination" or call it "extension") galled them in the teaching of St. Paul and of Jesus Christ. These were cheapening the holy faith, offering it on easy terms.

Before we criticise the Jews, see how easily we make the same mistake. We are always being told by clerics not to "popularise" Christianity, to maintain its traditional standards, to narrow the doorways into the Church. If people want the Christian faith, they must submit to whatever we personally consider essential tests — they must be personally "converted" if we are of one way of thinking, or "good church-people", if we are of another. Poor Samaritans, they are always with us and always being scolded, warned off the holy turf, treated as "heathen men and publicans".

1 CHRONICLES 21

58
THE DANGER OF STATISTICS

AFFECTION FOR HIS SUBJECT CAN be an advantage to a portrait painter; it is a doubtful asset to a biographer and a positive danger to a historian, particularly if admiration be added to affection. This is one of the great difficulties of "hagiography", writing about holy men and women. It is usually attempted by those who are already persuaded of the virtue and sanctity of their subject. Consequently, they are tempted to omit as probably false and certainly unsuitable anything that is not creditable to the person concerned, and to accept as true what is at best only a possibility. The Books of Chronicles are an example of this process. Written probably eight hundred years after the earliest events recorded, they are a deliberate attempt to reassess the story of the Books of Samuel and Kings with the hindsight of later centuries. Convinced of the dominating importance of the Law as then accepted, the authors of "Chronicles" rewrite history in such a way that the Law becomes the real hero of their books and all other human experiences of morality are subordinate to it. The "good" characters then must behave with uniform goodness — and that "goodness" will be expressed by acceptance of the precepts of the Law. Any stories that reflect discredit must be excised.

To see this process at work, we have only to compare the life of David as given in Chronicles and Samuel — and what devoted literalist interpreters of the Bible make of such comparison it is impossible to guess. Here are three obvious divergences. 1. The Census in Samuel is instigated by God, in Chronicles by Satan. 2. The numbers, in either case grossly inflated, do not tally. 3 The whole ceremonial side of the incident is, in the second version, vastly expanded and the price of the land inflated beyond even a speculator's dreams.

In fact, comparison of the live stories shows just exactly how all hagiography — not least the semi-history of the Old Testament — is almost inevitably developed away from truth towards romantic deception. Equally, such comparison suggests that the earlier stories have a good large kernel of original fact which was, by reason of its awkward truth, disagreeable to later editors and compilers.

But what kind of truth can lie behind so curious a story as this? Why should Census-taking be regarded as somehow "sinful", and why should it have incurred even in an imaginative connexion so ferocious a penalty? Is there any conceivable modern parallel to a situation which seems both crazy and cruel?

Now the purpose of the Census was evidently military — it was carried out by the commander-in-chief and his staff, the persons numbered were military effectives, the commander-in-chief himself would have liked (verse 3) to have seen the already immense numbers monstrously inflated. What the unhappy quarter-masters would have thought of such a suggestion is not recorded.

It is to be supposed, therefore, that any such calculation of assets was what the Greeks would have called *"hubris"*, an act of presumption. It is the old sin of pride, the belief that all these material assets are rock solid, that a man can do what he likes with his own. This leads not only to a cold-blooded disregard of others, but to the belief in the moral justice of one's own power. "I am rich, and I am good. Therefore I shall use my power well : and the ways I use it are, of course, good ways. So I am above judgement and deserve every success. Those who oppose me must be morally evil, so it is right for me to crush them."

It is not, then, the taking of a census in itself that is morally wrong — after all, the Gospels have something to say about counting the cost — but the attitude of mind which suggests a census. It is the embryo of power politics, ancient and modern — the preparation before invasion, the decision to smash the possible enemy whilst he is still weak, the abdication of moral responsibility and the surrender to self-importance.

EZRA 9

59

MIXED MARRIAGES

THERE IS NO DOUBT THAT THE two books, called in our Bible "Ezra" and "Nehemiah", were originally one continuous work. They are still, in fact, shown as such in the standard Roman Catholic version of the Bible, under the name of 1 Esdras. But to discover just how the two parts are related, and what is the historical background which unites them is quite another question. Roughly speaking, they give an account (the only Hebrew one we possess) of the two hundred years between 537 and 337 B.C., and of what was happening to Judaism and its belief during that time. All sorts of attempts have been made to break down this account into chronological sections and to separate the various strands of personal narrative and recorded history. One such — and it has fairly good evidence to support it — suggests that *Nehemiah* rebuilt the city and reorganised it politically, and that, a generation later, he was followed by *Ezra*, a religious reformer whose work is described in the last chapters of Nehemiah as well as in the last chapter of Ezra. Those interested in the quite extraordinarily difficult problems of historical reconciliation involved will find plenty of material for study and argument.

But the question of racial purity emphasised in the section we have chosen is topical enough, in all conscience. Even the weather (verse 9) has an appropriate touch about it.

Are mixed marriages desirable or not? Do they, as the Hebrews feared, corrupt the integrity of a nation and the vitality of its faith? Or are they essential if we are ever to discover a way to human brotherhood? Incidentally, note how it is assumed that even though a woman had neither rights nor liberties, she had still the influence to persuade her husband to accept her religious beliefs, as well as the chance to teach them to her children. Now to us, in an irreligious society, mixed marriages mean a racial rather than religious mixture. Although marriage between Christians of different denominations produces its own problems, these are problems within the one Christian family. Their common faith *ought* to mean that their marriage is more stable, however strong the points of difference in interpretation, than that of an agnostic and a Christian.

Much of our emotional attitude to the racially mixed marriage springs from the historical fact that, in the past, such relationships have often been those of military rape or colonial concubinage. Subconsciously we see in the marriage a representation of an evil situation — and therefore we reject it. This is particularly the case where there is a difference of colour. It is somehow then assumed that physical desire, of an "unhealthy" sort, must be the cause. It would be kinder and wiser to say that pity and even curiosity (as Shakespeare recognised) are more likely to be involved. And it is also true to say that in many such marriages both parties to the union have had to face so many problems and overcome so many difficulties that their love is not only "romantic" in the most traditional sense but also most fully tested and developed. Of course it is difficult to marry someone of different background, of different tradition and prejudice. (But this is so whatever their colour.) Of course it is difficult to face the possible slights and probable misunderstandings involved. But a happy marriage between two representatives of different races is the best possible evidence that understanding and good-will can unite the nations — whilst we hear much of the problems of the child of mixed nationality, we hear little of his no less remarkable possibilities. It is a wonderful thing to inherit two cultures, as of right, and to be ashamed of neither. This is splendidly established in the detective stories of Arthur Upfield, and in the life of their hero, an Inspector of white and aboriginal Australian parentage. If mixed marriages often go wrong, it is not so much because they are by nature impossible as because we give them so little chance of going right.

NEHEMIAH 2; 4. 13–23 and 5

60

THE MAN AND HIS WORK

THE BOOK OF NEHEMIAH HAS this in common with Esther and David, that it tells the story of how "Local Boy (or Girl) Makes Good at Court". It is as well to remember that this was one of the only roads open to any ambitious boy who chanced to be born of a captive or enslaved race. History shows how many of the most successful of court officers were, in fact, freedmen of this sort. Any society which wants to survive needs to make use of the best abilities latent in its people. This means that there must be channels available for promotion, irrespective of background. It may be done by open examination (as in ancient China or modern Britain), it may be done by personal selection, by personnel department, by birth, by bribery — or by luck.

Nehemiah combines personality, courage, and decisiveness. His own prosperity does not make him forgetful of his people and his faith. And when the needs of both are brought to his attention, he first says his prayers, and then takes action. The action he takes is related to his opportunity. In other words, he uses his position at court, where quite clearly he is liked by both king and queen, to attract their attention to his unaccustomed gloom. This leads them to make enquiry about him, and this in turn gives him a chance to get royal permission to go back to Jerusalem, and also royal authority to requisition building materials when he gets there.

Arrived at Jerusalem, he finds a situation bad enough to make anyone give up and go home. The local bigwigs are hostile, the ravaged city in an appalling condition, his own party and the established settlers extremely pessimistic.

But Nehemiah understands the problem of morale. He realises that he has somehow got to give his people pride in themselves and confidence in each other. So he marks out a perimeter into sections and sets them all to build, each within his own vocational or family group. At once local and family patriotism are engaged. Clergy, goldsmiths, doctors, even (chapter 3, verse 12) daughters alongside their fathers, are hard at work. One man (verse 20) is commended for devotion to the job, an aristocratic group (verse 5) are censured because they felt manual work beneath them. But everybody lends a hand — and anyone who has shared, say, in the rebuilding of the Abbey at Iona will agree that there is nothing which so consolidates interest as an actual share in manual labour, however unskilled.

As the walls go up, their neighbours and enemies at first sneer, and then lay information — to be followed by open violence. It is at this stage that Nehemiah really proves his quality. He divides his forces, so that during working hours half of them are armed and standing-to permanently, whilst the other half are working on the wall under their protection. This was, incidentally, the method adopted by the Matabele Expedition which founded Rhodesia. Half cut a way for the wagons with axes, whilst half stood by with loaded rifles.

In addition, every mason and hodman had a weapon handy, and a signal system was organised to give instant alarm. The camp was rebuilt inside the perimeter of the rising walls, and everyone slept at the ready.

So the city begins to take shape — and a new problem arises, a class system of rich and poor, debtors and creditors. The wealthy have supplied the immigrants with the food and necessities they wanted, but have claimed as security the title to their farms and smallholdings, as well as a return in commodities. Nehemiah, by the sheer example of his own disinterested patriotism, as well as by the eloquence of which he was obviously a master, secures a cancellation of all these agreements. But no sooner is this settled than the enemy outside renew their undercover attack. First they plan the assassination of Nehemiah outside the city. Then they attempt blackmail. Next, a fifth column is suborned to spread alarm and despondency and weaken Nehemiah's influence (one of the enemy, Tobiah, had a number of relatives-in-law in high places : later on (chapter 13, verses 4 to 9) he is even discovered to have been given a sort of "grace-and-favour" apartment in the temple itself!)

But all this Nehemiah survives, and stays long enough to see the city rising from the ashes within its restored walls, the temple worship re-established and properly endowed, the integrity of the nation reasserted after far too many mixed marriages had corrupted it, and even Sabbath observance given priority over commercial undertaking. A remarkable man, Nehemiah, and a good patron saint for anyone to choose if he has to undertake reform and restoration. He was fearless, yet sympathetic; never lost his nerve or his faith : knew always what was sensible and possible as well as what was right. His epitaph is written in the final words of his book, "Remember me, O my God, for good".

61

ANTI-SEMITISM PUNISHED

ANTI-SEMITISM IS A SOCIAL disease, like syphilis, of long standing. Like syphilis, it can be avoided by those of sense and morality. To explain it completely is impossible. There is about it an element of resentment of those who work harder than we do — of suspicion of those whose cultural values are often more advanced — of envy of those whose family life is more stable — of withdrawal from those who are on occasion more apt than we are to exhibition, whether of emotions or possessions. Sometimes supposed to be the creation of Christians, it antedates the life and death of one who was himself a Jew, whose faith was chiefly preached by another Jew.

Now the Book of Esther is an account, a vivid but neither specially moral nor specially religious account, of a Jewish-Gentile clash. Probably included in the Bible only as explanation of the origin of the feast of Purim (see chapter 9), it tells the story of how a royal concubine was able to use her influence to protect her own people and bring total destruction upon their enemies. Chapter 3, verse 8 gives in brief the classic statement of the anti-semite — that there is "a certain people . . . dispersed among the people in all provinces . . . and their laws are diverse from all people". In other words, "there are a lot of them . . . you find them everywhere . . . they are different from us". The next verse (verse 9) suggests a further reason. "They are rich: if we kill them, there's money in it." Yet verse 15 reminds us that even in Shushan there were sensible people, who could see neither justice nor sense in persecution — and were "perplexed".

Chapter 4 contains perhaps the one really uplifting passage in the book. This is the moment in verse 14 when her cousin, Mordecai, reminds Esther of her chance, of her responsibility; "who knoweth whether thou art come to the kingdom for such a time as this?"

Such a situation can occur in a wide variety of contexts. It forecasts the simple problem — "must I risk all I've got on a matter of principle?" It can be petty, petty as with the person who feels that prosperity means giving up all their old friends for fear they should be a social hindrance. It can be a desperately hard decision — as that of the politician who feels in honesty compelled to wreck his career by voting against his party. But the moral of Esther is surely this, that the real quality of greatness is shown in readiness to sacrifice oneself upon a matter of right and wrong. It is our habit to suppose that the great point about power is first to get and keep it — and then to see how we can use it, according to our own standards of what is right. Compromises, we accept, must be made if we are to keep power, but we believe that we ourselves, even with such compromises, are better to be trusted than the next man.

But here is a girl who sees that there comes a time when absolutely everything for which we've worked and hoped may have to be risked — and risked for what can seem mere foolishness of scruple or an unnecessary loyalty. It is better in those moments to lose the whole world, so hardly gained, than to lose our souls.

JOB
(summary)

62

DOUBTFUL COMFORT

JOB HAD THREE FRIENDS. WHEN his troubles came upon him, his friends came too. Unlike a good many of us, they *did* come. How well we know the situation. Poor old George is in hospital again — it is an all-day journey to reach him, and visiting hours are almost impossible. Tom has lost his job, and he's got no savings to tide him over. We should feel awkward meeting him, knowing what we've got put by ourselves — besides, he might even want to make a touch. So we agree that it is really kinder not to bother him; when we see him in the High Street we can always slip in to the chemist and avoid an embarrassing meeting. But Job's friends stood by him

— and when they did come, they had the sense just to be quiet. All the good — and more — of a friendly visit in other people's time of trouble is undone by slick words of comfort. A man whose small son died tragically after a long illness described the kind of help some of his acquaintances offered. They talked of "God the gardener, picking the fairest rose-bud"; they told him how, years hence, he would know "it has all been for the best". They indicated that the child was much better in the divine keeping than when he was cherished by his parents. In fact, they were *trivial,* and their petty triviality only insulted the heartbreak of the parents. Better at such a time to say nothing, to admit that there are no words or even reasons. Better just to show love and friendship.

So far then, the three friends set us all an example. Perhaps they overdid it a bit, spending a *week,* but at least they put their friend's trouble first and cancelled all their other activities and engagements. The real difficulty begins when they start to *speak.* Consider the arguments they put forward.

Eliphaz (chapter 4) reminds Job how often he himself has urged people to faith and courage. What about showing these qualities himself *now?* All life, he adds, is perilous and unsure, but — in chapter 5 — if he holds on, it will be all right, Job will find.

Bildad, in chapter 8, suggests that everything has a cause, and that there must be *some* reason for what has befallen his friend. Zophar (chapter 11) is equally smug. Behave yourself now with propriety, accept your troubles with proper humility, and all will be well.

Job finds it hard to tolerate windy piety of this sort. He is a Prometheus figure challenging heaven — an honest man, who just wants to know "why". Only let me get at God, he says, and put my case to him. After all, he's got it all his own way : his are the big battalions, and the final decisions : why not then be prepared to put his case to Job and help him see the reason for it all? Better not be born at all, says poor Job, than face a life of idiot injustice.

Eliphaz (chapter 15) is shocked. "Are you arguing with *God?*" he says, appalled. "And who do you think you are," adds Bildad (chapter 18), "who want life explained to you?" In chapter 22 back comes Eliphaz, pointing out that God owes nothing to Job, anyway. (He is not, by implication, much concerned with him.) Apology is what's wanted. Say you're sorry, even if you don't know what for, and leave it to him to put things right.

This leads to chapter 23, Job's tremendous appeal. In the next chapter he states his belief in moral rectitude. He will *not* compromise his faith in reason and justice: he will *not* accept the idea of a God who cannot be approached in terms of equity and understanding. Verse after verse, of superb poetry, looks back to his days of happiness and — he still maintains — of moral virtue as well. And with his final assertion of this, at the end of chapter 31 the three "comforters" at last are silent.

So far the story has been a dialogue, in structure resembling a Greek tragedy. All the action takes place off stage at the beginning; since then we have had nothing but to-and-fro argument. Now there enters a new figure, a young man, representative of the "New Theology". Clearly the author means us to see the cogency of his argument — though, in fact, it is extremely hard so to do. He begins (chapter 33) by saying to Job, "If you want someone to argue with, argue with *me*". You say God doesn't communicate with you? But he does. First, in dreams (a very modern suggestion this one) and second, through the good and bad of everyday life.

But, after all, God is not subject to your ideas of justice. He is transcendent, supreme. If you cannot understand the natural laws of his creation, how can you hope to understand the moral laws of his behaviour?

And then, in chapter 38, comes the "theophany", the God-appearance (again, as in Greek drama). It is magnificent, but it's not really an answer. All it says is "You must trust me, as you cannot know me". And Job is silent. But his fortunes are restored, his herds increased, his friends (chapter 42, verse 11) bring financial help — which would probably have been much more useful earlier on — his daughters are beautiful and his age interminable.

The theme, then, of the book is truly the essence of tragedy,

I

the story of the good man who suffers — who wants, above all, not freedom from suffering, but a reason for it. He wants to know that he's still right to trust and believe in God, and that all morality is not mockery, all faith not self-delusion. And he comes to find a personal relationship with God (with a God who speaks himself, not through anyone else), and with that relationship his faith returns. This is, in a way, a prologue to the passion story of Christ, where the same question is asked. Why should the innocent suffer? In the Book of Job, the answer is that we must leave the answer to God and love him still. In the Gospel, we can see God himself confronting the question, and identifying himself with all those whose pain compels them to ask it.

JOB 1. 6–12 and 2. 1–17

63

THE DEVIL IT IS

THERE HAVE BEEN MANY IMAGES or projections of personalised evil, a number of which have no relation to the Bible. That shaggy figure with horns and a tail so popular with fancy dress creators is probably a reminiscence of the fertility gods of the field and wood, damned by the new faith, and held up to execration. Literally driven underground, he leaves his authority over bird and beast, to rule in hell. But his piping has still a certain charm, though his "panic" terror is now more potent, and his magic very black. At all events, he has no place in the Bible, unless alongside the Golden Calf.

At the same time, one of the Bible expressions of utter evil, the dragon, emblem of ruthless power, has disappeared from our thought-images, and lingers on only when defeated by St. Michael and St. George. Another Bible figure, the serpent, has been sadly confused. In Genesis he is simply a "beast of the field", though the cleverest of them all. He tempts Adam and Eve with the thought of new knowledge and new power — and he and they both suffer for it. But he is *not* a supernatural being, and the penalty dealt out to him is expressed simply in the terms of dishonour and of dislike, rather than of any eternal judgement.

There remain, if these be excepted, two pictures of the devil as a supernatural created being. In one case the being has stooped from his high estate, and wars through pride against God; on the other, he is still part of the divine entourage but functions within it like a mediaeval jester. He is the cynic, the debunker, the eternal wise-guy.

Reference to the first is to be found in Isaiah 14, verse 12 — though this may be nothing more than a reference to a stellar deity of the pagan world; to the second, in the opening sections of Job, and (very briefly) in the first verses of the third chapter of Zechariah.

What then is this "Satan"? He is, as was said above, the tester, the acid which proves the true gold or destroys the false. In this sense he is a "tempter", but his temptations are simply his way of testing. Nor can he tempt without divine permission, even if he argues very ingeniously in order to win that permission. It is hard, too, not to suppose that he takes a real pleasure in the subtle ferocity of the sufferings he devises.

Now such a picture of the devil was devised in order to reconcile the absolute power of God, which to the Jews was his characteristic, with human suffering. Indeed, the whole of the Book of Job is a magnificent and sombre statement of man's case against God, of the despair of the righteous who suffer and their longing at least for an explanation. The first explanation offered is simply that suffering comes to try the reality of our faith and the integrity of belief. Are we in this for what we can get or have already got? Is honesty only to be chosen because it is the best-paying policy?

Satan the tester is an ingenious way of explaining the existence of human injustice and human sufferings, though it is scarcely one which today convinces us. Yet within it there does lurk the truth that no suffering of *necessity* destroys goodness — indeed that goodness emerges the more triumphant. Above and beyond the bowed head of Job hangs a man upon a cross.

64

A SHEEP'S SONG

PROBABLY THE MOST POPULAR poem in the world — and apparently the work of a sheep. At least, the writer writes from the point of view of a sheep. And his words have, over and again, been set to popular music, as in "Crimond" or "Brother James' Air" : have been paraphrased by poets like Addison, hymn-writers like Baker : have been the comfort of millions, the inspiration of thousands : have been illustrated, expanded, translated in every language and technique imaginable. If there is one psalm in the collection that really is the work of David, surely this must be it.

For it describes a day in the shepherd's life — though all from the sheep's point of view. He is, of course, an Eastern shepherd, whose job it is to lead his flock from pasture to water-hole, to guard them by day from wolf or bear, and to see them folded safely by night. The sheep trust him. He is *their* shepherd, and known to them. They bear his brand-mark, and follow him to the oasis. In verse 3 we hear of the stray brought back and the lost lamb found. In verse 4 they go through dangerous defiles, where the wild beasts lurk. Here the shepherd needs his cudgel as well as his crook, and the sheep crowd close behind him for company and protection.

But he brings them in the next verse safely to their next camping-ground. Here "sheep may safely graze" even with wolves on the prowl and the jackals howling. There is good drinking water : and scratches and wounds can be washed and smeared with oil or tar. The sixth verse suggests the total protection given to the sheep, behind as well as before. Though their shepherd goes in front, they are guarded from danger on every side. If Eastern shepherds had used dogs, it would have been tempting to see in this verse a picture of God's goodness and mercy as literally "dogging" our footsteps. In this verse, too, the flock come safe at last to fold, and end in the protection of their master's cave.

This psalm has become so established a part of our religious background that we forget how revolutionary were its ideas when first stated. For it speaks of God not as monarch, supreme authority, giver of laws, master of nations — but as caring, loving, guiding. And it sees the sheep themselves, not only as units of wealth or as staples of the food supply, but as entities capable of emotion. There is a good deal in the Old Testament about the work of the shepherd — but very little about the life of the sheep. It is as though someone today were to write a hymn in which the hens spoke with love and trust about the poultry-farmer. If this idea seems ludicrous, it may be because of the way we treat our poultry, rather than because such a relationship is of necessity ludicrous. Would David, for instance, have force-fed captive geese to torture their livers into producing *foie gras?*

PSALMS 69 and 22

65

PSALMS OF DESOLATION

SOME OF THE PSALMS ARE SONGS of praise: some are history set to verse, in the way of a Scots ballad: some seem to be just a musical snarl of hatred. And these are the hardest of all for us to understand. How, we say, can anyone imply, in the course of a church service, that a special blessing will be bestowed on the slaughter of enemy infants (Psalm 137, verse 9), or that God will do us a kindness by refusing to forgive (Psalm 109, verses 14 and 15). Yet it is as well for us who have never, as a nation, suffered terribly to remember that these are the songs and prayers of the persecuted. These are, in fact, psalms which might have been sung, not *by* us, but *about* us. This is the sob of the ghetto, the cry of the slave, the voice of all suffering as it asks, "How long, O Lord, how long?"

It is quite a good discipline to read these in this light, and to think again about our attitudes and responsibilities. It is probably useful, too, to see just what are the sins the Psalmist condemns most fiercely: deceit is one, cruelty another, disloyalty to friends a third. Pride is one, and greed, empty-headedness (the impertinence of folly), lack of compassion, conspiring against the weak, are others. All these are evils we know well enough: perhaps the danger is that they are so easy to detect and condemn in other people — so easy to conceal from ourselves.

But there is one aspect of the "hate-psalms" which we also need to remember. In almost every case the cataloguing of the persecutors' sins is linked with a prayer of total trust and commitment. The agonised writer may ask God to deal with his enemies; he does not ask a particular blessing on the weapons which he himself proposes to use. Practical and hard-headed people as we like to feel ourselves, we are very fond of using the prayer in *The Critics*

"Grant us our ends
And sanctify, whatever means we use to gain them".

This prayer of trust is not limited to the immediate speaker. In this psalm, for instance, it spills over to all his people and identifies them with him.

Now when we turn from Psalm 69 to 22, we discover something else. First: the element of cursing and the prayer for revenge are both gone. Here are the enemies — but there is no condemnation of them. Second: no longer is the golden promise of justification limited to Israel: now it is extended to all the dwellers upon earth, all those that are, and all that shall be.

And when we come to examine the details, we know at once that "we have been here before". Surely these are the particulars of Calvary — the stripping of garments, the diceing of soldiers, the nails hammered home, the jeering crowd? More than that, the very words with which it begins are the words Christ used in his desolation. We know how much Christ loved the psalms and how he found in them (Luke 24, verse 44) reverence to his own life and mission. May it not be that in the dark loneliness of the Cross he discovered to the full the meaning of this psalm, and knew that now he was completely fulfilling his intended purpose? This was the duty and unique responsibility

134

of the Messiah: now in him all the weeping, all the sad com-
plaining, all the cries of despair found their answer. Now men
knew what God was like, for he was here before them on the
Cross. The divine nature was declared, so that the "people that
shall be born" — even 1900-odd years later — would one day
understand it. Not the despairing cry of a man feeling himself
betrayed by the God whose son he had believed himself to be,
not the warning to his friends that the faith he had shared with
them was false, but the final identification of himself with the
promised Messiah, the final acceptance of his role of suffering
that others may be saved.

PSALM 150

66

"PRAISE, MY SOUL THE KING OF HEAVEN"

PERHAPS "PRAISE" IS THAT
aspect of worship which is most misunderstood. Petition — asking for benefits — we can easily appreciate: penitence, even in
its secular form of remorse, is a frequent part of our ordinary
experience: thanksgiving, agreeable to say, is also an expression
of feeling common to most of us. But what do we mean by
"praise"? Do we believe that God enjoys our adulation, that he
is one of those tyrannic figures who depend on flattery, that
unless we use the proper forms of approach he will turn a deaf
ear to anything else which we have got to say? Such a belief
may be appropriate in the case of those false gods which are
only a projection of our own power-complex or sense of in-
security. It is wildly inappropriate if we are thinking of a father-
child relationship — "Daddy, how big and strong you are; will
you give me a shilling?" is not our ideal of the way our children
should approach us.

The "Lord of heaven and earth" certainly doesn't need our
praise to make him feel good: he is good already. Nor does he

insist on appropriate politeness before he will enter into conversation : he hears while we are yet speaking, and knows our petitions before we ask.

But the activity of praise is not intended to benefit God — which is, anyway, impossible — but to help the worshipper. C. S. Lewis, in his *Reflexions on the Psalms,* has made this admirably clear.

The purpose of praise, he says, is to get our order of values right. It is a recognition of what is good, a reinforcement of our awareness of good and evil, beauty and ugliness.

After all, if we are discussing, say, modern architecture, we shall properly spend much of our time in listing those buildings which we think should be admired, in explaining why we think them admirable. Praise, in this sense, is affirmation of belief. Now such affirmation is akin to trust. We praise him, though he slay. Praise, when all is dark and dreary, praise, when we have little reasonable ground for cheerfulness — such praise is really a statement of our belief in the love of God and our steadfast committal of ourselves and all we care about into his hands.

Perhaps the nearest human comparison to praise of this sort is to be heard in the exchanges of lovers. Each knows of the other's love : each is absolutely assured of it. Yet they will continue to find delight in murmuring, "I love you, darling," and be perfectly satisfied with this as a significant form of conversational interchange.

To this degree, our praise of God is simply putting into words, for our own comfort and pleasure, our own love for him and appreciation of his overwhelming love for us. It's something *we* want to do, not something he demands as tribute from us.

Finally, praise is not only recognition of worth, not only the expression of our heart's conviction and our soul's desire, it is also a form of identification with others.

There are few, if any, of the great songs of praise, from the *"Te Deum"* itself to Lyte's hymn whose opening words are quoted above, which do not invite other people to join in. The *"Benedicite"* is a splendid case in point, and one which it would be a useful exercise to bring up to date. "Ye oysters and buffaloes," sang a little boy, "bless ye the Lord" ; "Ye underground trains and hover-buses, bless ye the Lord"; not only Ananias, Azarias and Misael, but Tom, Dick, and Harry should praise him too.

Praise, from this point of view, is recognition. It is seeing the hand of God even in the unlikely. It is noticing the peacock colour in the iridescence of an oil-stain on muddy cobbles, and it is finding harmony in the thunder of machinery in Wigan as well as in that of the waves in Fingal's cave.

So we praise God in all human fellowship: we praise him in orchestra and ballet: we praise him in public worship and in daily life.

"Let everything that hath breath — praise the Lord."

THE BOOK OF PROVERBS 8. 1–36 and 31. 10–31

67

MARRIAGE: CRACKER MOTTOES

THIS IS A QUITE IMPOSSIBLE book for use in church. All the best parts of it are disconnected verses, from the dire warning against being jolly at breakfast (chapter 27, verse 14) to the wise comment on contentment (chapter 15, verse 17), from recognition of the real values of life (chapter 13, verse 7) to the doom of the frequenters of brothels (chapter 9, verses 17 to 18).

There are, however, two themes which give some unity to the book and they are expressed in the two passages selected.

The first is the contrast between "wisdom" and "folly". And here wisdom is interpreted in two ways. The first corresponds to our virtue of prudence, or self-control. It is the virtue of the man who does not waste his time or his money, who is not envious of others, who knows how to behave with those who are richer and more important than himself, as with those who are less so. He works hard, is respectful to his parents, picks his friends with care, and is moderate in his drinking (see chapter 23, verses 20, 21). He minds his own business, spreads no gossip (chapter 26, verses 17 to 22), is politically conservative (chapter 24, verse 21) and merciful to the needy and even to his enemy (chapter 25, verses 21 and 22).

But the second meaning of "wisdom" is quite different. Here "wisdom" becomes personified, the Holy Wisdom of God (as it was honoured in the name of the great church of Constantinople ("*Hagia Sophia*"). The feminine name suggests indeed something akin to a feminine goddess who is to be wooed like a mortal woman. This "Lady Wisdom" is described in chapter 1, verse 20, and continues up to chapter 3, verse 26. She comes upon the scene again in the first of our passages, and is to be identified with the living and creating power of the Almighty himself. It was this concept of wisdom which gave T. E. Lawrence the title for his book on his Arabian campaigns (chapter 9, verse 1) — for this is the driving spirit of artist and scholar, soldier and statesman, of all who try to discover or to create order and harmony. Such an interpretation of wisdom is contained in the compound "philosophy" — literally "the love of wisdom" — where *"Sophia"* ("wisdom") means the totality of life itself. A whole group of Bible books share this theme, and are therefore often known as the "Wisdom Literature" : they seem to have some affinity to the thought of St. John, and particularly to his doctrine of Christ, the *"logos"* or "Creating Word of God".

The second passage has this in common with the first, that it too deals with a feminine being. But this time it is a very human one, a wife and a mother. Now there are few passages in the whole Bible which can be said to glorify marriage. There is a certain amount of reference to youthful devotion, rather more to adulterous passion, but very little to happy and stable family life. Even this chapter is rather more concerned with the niceties of good housekeeping than with the love and joy of husband and wife. But it is still a picture of a woman who, in a predominantly masculine society, has made her own place by her character and ability and, even if she has no legal power, rules, one may believe, by knowledge of human psychology and by awareness of her husband's foibles. The present age focusses upon marriage as the legitimising of physical passion and accepts the drying up of such passion as authority for the abrogation of the marriage. To the people of earlier ages, the strength of marriage lay in its sense of working partnership. This was far too precious to be hazarded by the to-and-fro of sexual desire, and might therefore be separated from it. A man took concubines almost at whim — but a good wife was a lifelong treasure, and indeed might well, like wine, improve with age.

ECCLESIASTES 12 (and other passages)

68

TOMORROW WE DIE

THE "FIG-LEAF" TENDENCY, THE writing-in of an improving moral so as to disguise the naked truth, is very strong in Ecclesiastes. In fact, the book becomes a truth, is very strong in Ecclesiastes. In fact, the book becomes a disconnected dialogue, in which the first writer, a poet, "vanity" — which means, literally, "emptiness". He shares the point of view of those who can see no meaning in anything, but simply a sequence of events which chance to occur, and then, having occurred, go on endlessly recurring (chapter 1, verses 1 to 11). *Knowledge* (chapter 1, verses 12 to 18), *Pleasure* (chapter 2, verses 1 to 11), *Work* (chapter 2, verses 18 to 23), *Riches* (chapter 6, verses 1 and 2), even *Justice* (chapter 8, verses 14 to 17) all lead only to frustration.

This would make it a book of almost total cynicism were it not for the second voice in the dialogue, a part possibly written in by some pious commentator who felt that, without it, the book could have no moral value whatever. This second voice usually utters smug clichés as to rewards and punishments (chapter 2, verses 24 to 26). Chapter 3, however, begins with a splendidly phrased presentation of the concept that life *does* have purpose and order, though it rapidly turns aside into a sorrowful identification of man and the beasts that perish (verse 16, onwards).

Again and again in the succeeding chapters we meet this

desperate assertion of purpose and justice (e.g. chapter 5, verses 18 to 20, chapter 8, verses 12 to 13) over against the nihilism of the first writer. At last the dialectic resolves itself. The final synthesis (chapter 9, onwards) suggests acceptance of good, whenever and however it comes, along with endurance of trouble — but all without over-much hope of good to come (chapter 11, verses 7 to 10). The last chapter is one of the loveliest descriptions of old age ever to be written. The very fact that it is written without thought of a life to come — and therefore without hope — gives it a special dignity and stoic splendour (which is only weakened by the very last verse, surely an echo of the Second Voice at its smuggest).

Each physical and mental symptom of age is accurely reproduced. Failing muscles, man sans eyes, and sans teeth, cracked voice, cracked nerve, white hair, stumbling gait, weary back — and at the last, dust and ashes. Even wisdom itself, even communication of truth, becomes but a "weariness to the flesh".

This is a magnificent book, and in its seesawing between a desperate search for some *meaning* and a pious assertion that this meaning is to be found within the most conventional morality it illustrates a position that is common enough in our experience. For we find scientists and intellectuals, trained thinkers, who provide themselves with a religion of the most assertive and unthinking sort — Christian or Communist — as though to counterbalance the independence of their secular thought. But is this good? We can understand well enough the temptation of a religion of authority; how attractive, we sometimes feel, to be told what you must or must not believe, to be so sure that you and you alone are right. Yet of these two voices which one really comes closest to speaking the Word of God — that which tries so hard to discover meaning though without success or that which can always offer an easy answer? Our day and age has found in Kierkegaard and Bonhoeffer encouragement to look for a God who is not to be identified *anywhere* because he is *everywhere,* who is only to be found when we despair of looking, who is waiting to meet us when we at last turn home. But without the seeking and the despair we should never have realised our necessity or his presence.

69

PROFANE LOVE

THE WHOLE BOOK IS SUGGESTED
for reading at a sitting, since it is hard to believe that anyone
who begins on this passionate and dramatic love poem will stop
before reaching the end. It is, in fact, one of the books of the
Bible which greatly need to be lifted out of its traditional pattern of chapter and verse and printed instead in dramatic form.
Such a form is that of a "Pastoral", a story of rustic romance,
punctuated with songs and dances. (Perhaps our modern
"musical comedy" is its nearest surviving relative.)

There are at least three rôles in this one. First, the heroine, a
sunburned country girl, in love either with a prince who plays,
in the traditional way, at being a shepherd, or a shepherd who
is to her a prince. They woo each other amongst the green
shadows of the vineyards, they quarrel and part, they half-die
of grief at separation, they come together again — all in the
traditional formula "boy meets girl, boy loves girl : boy quarrels
with girl : boy makes up with girl". And in the background is
the chorus, feminine and attractive, no doubt, as are all the best
choruses — the "daughters of Jerusalem".

It is a simple and pleasant exercise to sort out the various
parts. In chapter 1, for instance, the girl conducts a dialogue
with the chorus, whilst chapter 6 is a duet for the two lovers.

Now whilst this is a most moving and romantic drama, it is
openly and unashamedly an account of passionate physical love
and its fulfilment. It may indeed in origin be linked with all the
fertility traditions of springtime, the ritual marriage of earth
and sky. It appears, amongst the more "spiritual" books of the
Bible, like a magnificently naked man striding into a congrega-
tion of Sunday-clad citizens.

Our forefathers, aware of this, did their best with the little
italicised sub-headings they wrote in the column-heads and in
the chapter prefixes. We are to think of this duet, they say

apprehensively, as a dialogue between Christ and his Church. This is "sacred" love, and not "profane".

We are inclined to laugh at this as a form of prudery, like putting trouser-legs on tables or fig leaves on statues. But it is also, perhaps, a groping after a real truth. All love is of God and "he that loveth is born of God, and knoweth God". For many people their first — for some their only — experience of love is in human terms. Human love has always some physical element in it: after all, we all like to be in the physical presence of those we love. And physical love at its best is a desire to share in identity, by a mutual giving and receiving. Each of the two finds delight in each of these two expressions of sentiment. (At its worst, physical love is a unilateral taking, the desire to possess and to dominate.)

In physical love, therefore, divine love is at least partially and potentially revealed. And this affinity or identity is made clear in some parallel manifestations of both. For instance, persons can "fall in love", being suddenly and totally absorbed in desire for each other. In the same way, they can be "converted", becoming suddenly and totally aware of the love of God and of their need for him. Those who have known a sudden experience of either sort tend to believe that such experience is the only valid one, and to question the genuineness of all other kinds.

But equally people can grow into love, coming by degrees to recognise the significance of a relationship whether towards God or another human being. Such a relationship is as true as — and sometimes more enduring than — the previous one and often is the final stage of which the more violent one is the predecessor.

William James' classic *Varieties of Religious Experience* makes this plain: it is restated, in its parallel with sexual love, in William Wylie's *Pattern of Love*. The Song of Solomon, then, is rightly included in the Bible, just as physical love is rightly included in all thinking about love — for the Bible deals with life both as it is, and as it should be. Physical love is part of life as it is, and the right recognition and use of it are essential to life as it should be.

70

TRINITY OF HOLINESS

THE PROCESS OF INSPIRATION seems always to be much the same, whether in art or in religion. There is, first, revelation of truth. Second, a sense of total personal inadequacy to convey it. Third, an acceptance of a commission, and the discovery of power given to carry it out. Fourth — and subsequently — sad recognition of our failure to use that power properly, and to make real to others the splendour revealed to oneself.

Isaiah was a devoted churchman, and so his vision takes place in a church, in the great temple itself. We can be so impressed with the human interest and aesthetic glory of our great cathedrals that we forget to think of them essentially as revelations of God. Yet unless he is revealed intelligently through them they fail in their purpose. They exist, not for themselves or for us, but that we may find God in and through them.

This vision of God is accompanied by archangels, and by all the circumstances of an earthquake. It is the moment of truth for Isaiah, that moment which may at any time confront any one of us, when we see real goodness (even in a human being) and have the grace to be ashamed of ourselves. How much more when the vision is of infinite goodness. The greater the vision, the greater the shame of our unworthiness.

There follows the gift of fire. Fire was the emblem of God's glory, but it was a fire which — as in Moses' vision of the burning bush — illumined without destroying. This glory is imparted to the prophet. The flame touches his lips, to show that it is through his words that he will render his appointed service. But even so there is no compulsion. He is chosen and called — but he is free to refuse the call.

If this is the pattern of inspiration, it is also the pattern of vocation. A man has his own vision of God — perceived, if his vocation is to holy orders, as God within his Church. But at first he is overwhelmed by the sense of his own inadequacy, as well, perhaps, as by distrust of the visible expression of that Church. He sees little sign of seraphic glory in the "unclean lips" of gossiping pious women, platitudinous clerics, or pompous official pronouncements. But the call still sounds. There's need of men, however incapable : "I'll go," he cries, "send me".

The rest of the chapter may seem as true now as it was when it was written. People seem deliberately determined to reject the truth that would enlighten and the love that would help. They just don't want to be different, to consider any claim that could endanger their self-satisfaction. "Thank you," they say, "we don't go to church, but we are as good as those that do."

We enjoy reading of other people's sins : we are reasonably generous when an appeal touches our hearts : we feel sure that God will understand that we're really too busy just now to think of him. Please call another day.

Yet the message must still be delivered, and if we are very lucky, says the last verse in the chapter, one person in ten will pay some attention !

ISAIAH II. 1–9

71

GIFTS OF THE SPIRIT

THE ANGLICAN CONFIRMATION service takes its central prayer from this splendid and royal prophecy. Royal because it is, of course, one of those passages in which it is promised that the future Messiah and King of Kings will be a descendant of David, the Shepherd King : splendid, because the kingliness of the Messiah is shown in the quality of his character and not in the power which will attend him. He is to be a king who brings peace, ending for ever even the blood-hunger of wolf and leopard, the two most ferocious of all the beasts of prey — as the lion and the bear are two of the most powerful, and the snake the most deadly.

This is a king who cannot be deceived by lying report, or fooled by surface appearance. His word is mighty to save, and he will uphold the poor and down-trodden.

But the verse which the Prayer Book compilers chose for their theme is the second, and at first sight this seems to be merely a collection of words all having the same meaning. Wisdom — understanding — counsel, might ("ghostly strength" in the Prayer Book), knowledge, fear of the Lord ("godliness" in the Prayer Book) — and then fear on top of it all?

But it makes more sense if we think of these qualities as a kind of ladder of perfection, a whole variety of attributes all of which are needed to make up the good life. *Wisdom* may then be interpreted as the common-sense of everyday, the know-how of life, the technical ability we all of us need to do our job properly. Christians ought to be capable and competent to the very best of their potential, nor is piety any excuse for remediable ignorance. Our intellectual capacity is not ours to decide; but the use we make of it is very much our affair. Christians must learn to think — for it is thinking which leads to wisdom. But it is only the very first step on the way to full maturity. *Understanding* comes next. By "understanding" we mean the ability to enter into another person, to see matters through their eyes and share their feelings. So sympathy is one of its by-products. But it is much more than being ready to cry with them in sorrow or sing with them in joy. It is that perceptiveness of their powers for good or evil, that warmth and genuine concern which are so endearing when we find them in another person. These are nothing to do with intellect, but everything to do with understanding. So this power to get on terms with other people is a natural and beautiful mark of the Spirit.

Counsel is the third gift. "Counsel" means, surely, the ability to communicate ideas and feelings. It is the mark of the good actor, or artist, preacher or teacher. Some people have it in over-flowing quantity: some, by their own shyness or coldness, inhibit the power in themselves. But it is a quality which we ought to develop in ourselves and encourage in other people, in whatever form it may appear. Of course it can be ill-used; our modern world is full of corrupt propaganda. But this is a cor-

K

ruption of what ought to be good : the greater the power of communication, the worse the corruption, whether it is the painter painting for profit and not for the vision's sake, or the fashionable preacher giving people what they want to hear.

After "Counsel", *Ghostly strength*. This is the power to stand alone. Never was there a time in history when this was so much needed. True freedom relies upon this same power, the power to defy the tyranny of popular belief or militant dictatorship. "Ghostly strength" means being ready to make up our own mind as to what is right and to stick to it, once made. It means developing an independent judgement, the readiness to give our opinion before looking round the table to see how others are going to vote.

Then, *Knowledge*. This "knowledge" must surely be perception of truth, the awareness of value, the recognition of beauty. To acquire knowledge in this sense is to see God, for it is to discover his action and manifestation in every aspect of life. Such knowledge is sometimes called "purity of heart", or "the single eye". It is only won by much searching, much fighting, and probably much suffering. But it is a quality we can recognise in those who have acquired it.

It leads straight on to *Godliness* — not the milk-and-water pietism the word suggests, but "Godlikeness", the ability to reflect in human personality the glory of God. This is the mark of the saint, the people in whom we see what God is like, and rejoice at the sight. The saints may make us feel small — but they also make us feel good. Something of the light and joy of divinity shines through them, as it blazed in all its undimmed fire in Jesus Christ.

Last, and greatest, gift — *Fear*. Not fright, not panic, not timidity, but the recognition of our own weakness, which only the strongest are strong enough to recognise in themselves. For pride is the final temptation of the saint, pride which encourages a willingness to be led into temptation. It is the belief that we can manage in our own strength, that we have now accepted enough from God to stand alone, that we understand him so well that we can be trusted not to make mistakes. Because fear is the greatest gift of the Spirit, it comes here at the end of the list. Yet it sometimes happens that those who lack any other grace possess this one. It is the gift which enables us to be sorry and calls us to repentance — and it is at once the first and last of all the gifts of God. As pride is the most dangerous and persistent of sins, so humility — the fear of God — is its natural antidote.

ISAIAH 35 (cp. 11. 6–9)

72

NO RABBIT DISREGARDED

THE STRUCTURE OF ALL OLD Testament prophecy, in its long-term national application, is basically the same. It begins with *Denunciation,* either of collective (social) or individual wrong-doing. This is followed by *Punishment,* in which the here-and-now consequences of this wrong-doing are realistically depicted. Next is *Apocalypse* (= "unfolding"), which describes the intervention of God, often called "The Day of the Lord". Finally, *Encouragement,* in which either a faithful few ("the remnant") or the whole people are promised the restoration of their well-being and happiness.

Now these processes are seen as a long-term justification of "Righteousness". God is a god of goodness, who is affronted by the evil that men do. This evil at last produces its inevitable penalty, after which there is a new start with divine impetus. This goodness is always expressed in human terms. It is made visible in the behaviour of men, and is never related to the sufferings of animals or the experience of the natural world.

But anyone who looks at the natural world is bound to notice the degree of suffering which results from our participation in it, quite apart from our moral behaviour. This suffering is of two sorts. There is the suffering caused by "natural" process and by the process which is haphazard. The first may usually be escaped by careful study of the laws of nature, whereas the second is totally unpredictable. That is to say, a man may avoid the risk of lightning by never standing under a tree in a thunderstorm — which is prudence — but be struck down by a bolt out of an apparently clear sky, a happening which we rather oddly call an "Act of God". To set up a home on the side of a volcano may be foolish and invite disaster — but who can anticipate an earthquake? We may build our house on the strongest of rock — but an avalanche can still overwhelm it. The Old Testament attitude to such catastrophe usually hovers between a supposing that it *must* be the penalty for some unsuspected wrong-doing and the belief that God is unpredictable, anyway. What man must do is to obey the divine law and leave the rest to the creator's care.

But the greatest of the prophets were not satisfied with this. God's purpose would not be complete, they said, nor his kingdom come, until even the natural processes were tamed. There must be no deserts any more, no drought or famine : there must be no disease either, no physical frustration or shortcoming, no blind people, no cripples. The mark of the kingdom is this perfection of creation, a world in which men were good — yes — but the natural world was good, likewise.

There is still another sort of suffering, that which the animals inflict on each other. We do our best to explain this away, and to point out that when there is neither memory nor anticipation, fear at least is removed. Unfortunately, this just isn't true. We've seen how the ill-treated dog cringes, both remembering *and* anticipating; we've heard the squeal of the rabbit, the cry of the stuck pig. It may be the case that their consumption of each other does emphasise the mutual dependence of the creatures of our world — but it is still dreadful to see a sheep wasted through the attack of parasites.

Isaiah shared this feeling with us. To him the fulfilled purpose of God must mean the end of every sort of suffering. Not only the end of natural disasters, but the end of destructive instincts too. No longer will the snake coil and strike, or the carnivore lust for fresh blood. The ancient enmities of beast and bird will be fused in common good-will, and all creation rejoice together in peace and happiness.

It is this kingdom of peace which the Messiah will bring, since he will rule not only in the hearts of men, but as Lord also of the earth and sea. He will silence the winds, and put the waves to sleep. He will care for the sparrow, and be at home with the beasts of the field. Stanley Spencer painted a moving picture of "Christ loving the scorpion"; the scorpion, in the kingdom of God, will love man into the bargain!

ISAIAH 45. 5–12

73

I CREATE GOOD

THE PROBLEM OF EVIL IS INSEparable from any consideration of good. Is it, for instance, simply a lesser stage or phase of goodness, a falling-short of perfection? Then greater evil equals lesser good, until at last we reach total evil as a total negative, the absence of anything active and positive, resembling the "heat-death" of which physicists used to speak. Life then is "good" — and the more alive it is the better: death is "evil" — if by death we mean an absolute end to existence.

Those who hold such a view do not necessarily accept the existence of a god. They may believe, with Bergson, in a "Life Force"; they may believe in a "divine-man", a super-humanity which will one day emerge from the process of evolution; they may believe, as Bernard Shaw appears to have done, in a God who is himself developing out of the whole process — or perhaps in a God who will only be understood against the background of that process fully completed.

Such a view, often condemned as mere "humanism", is originally connected with the highest possible view of divinity, since it implies the ultimate total sovereignty of God and the ultimate and total elimination of evil. At the same time, it gives the highest possible value to human freedom — the right to reject God — and recognises that it is this freedom, when perverted, that gives its dynamic to evil. Freedom, in fact, is so potent a quality that it gives life, even a corrupt life, to the dead mass of negation. It still has the power of choice, even if it fails to use it.

But the power and right of choice is only expressed in its perfection when it is exercised in the direction of the Good. Perfect freedom is service to God, because it is the deliberate and devoted decision to do his will. This is, of course, expressed in the temptation of Christ — as its reverse is expressed in the fall of Adam and Eve. (This has sometimes been called a "Fall upwards", since it has been identified with the acceptance of freedom and of the power of intelligent choice — the "Knowledge of Good and Evil".)

Evolution, as we know it, the growth of life towards an increasing degree of self-awareness, an increasing ability to determine environment, an increasing ability to communicate with others, is therefore a potential for evil as well as for good. It becomes easier to hurt as well as to help, and the more life is integrated and in mutual communion, the more devastating that hurt can be. The hydrogen-bomb is one result of evolution, the logical end of one of the two roads offered to mankind.

Yet God accepted this as the price which man and God pay for the power of freedom. We can only believe, therefore, that the gift is worth the cost of it. For God "creates" evil the moment he gives to any being the power to differ from him, since all that is other than God's will is less than good and therefore already evil. Total denial of God's will would be total evil. And whilst we may be allowed to believe that no such total denial can ever actually come to pass, and that every created being will retain some small spark of its divine origin and be therefore susceptible of redemption, it is also worth noticing that a being totally evil has lost the power of choice which gives life. It is therefore "dead", in the fullest sense, it is a No-Being, and a No-Thing. Ultimate evil destroys life and so destroys itself.

Such a view avoids the romanticising of evil which is apt to occur when we ascribe positive and dynamic qualities to the bad. It is hard, for instance, to read *Paradise Lost* without feeling some sort of sympathy with Lucifer just because of his impressive personality. But if evil be nihilist, deadly, then —

just as God is the final expression of personality, so Satan must represent its complete disintegration. Literally, his name is "Legion" — because in him chaos is come again.

74

THE NATURE OF LEADERSHIP

EVERY READER OF COMMENTARIES about Isaiah will know that this book is the work of at least two men and possibly of several others. The first is the statesman prophet who encouraged King Hezekiah to stand firm when "The Assyrian came down like a wolf on the fold" (2 Kings 18). The second, whose section begins at chapter 40, is concerned with the theme of the Suffering Servant. Hitherto it had always been supposed that when the "Messiah", the promised divine king, should come, he would come as a conqueror, overthrowing the heathen nations and establishing a successful Jewish political kingdom. Full details were given, down to the very place where the final battle would be fought.

But Second-Isaiah is utterly revolutionary. The king who will come, he says, will come as a man among men, and a poor man at that. He will be despised, rejected even by his own people, judged, condemned and executed. Yet he will be fulfilling God's will even in this, and through his suffering and death the people will be delivered.

This astonishing idea is presented in its fullness in this particular chapter, but it can be set alongside the passages of "good news" (or, to use its Greek translation "Evangel") in chapter 40, verses 1 to 11; in chapter 52; in chapters 61 and 62. It is repeated in chapter 50, verses 4 to 9, chapter 42, verses 1 to 9, and chapter 61, verses 1 to 11 (the passage chosen by Christ for the text of his first recorded sermon).

Modern Judaism has accepted these same passages as applicable, not to the Messiah as an individual, but to the whole

Jewish race, and has seen its national sufferings as part of its divine destiny.

These same passages are interleaved with others scarcely less remarkable, some of which promise hope and salvation not to the Jews only, but to Gentiles as well (chapter 60, verses 1 to 9, chapter 66, verses 18 to 23). Others repeat the regular prophetic warning that God is better served by social righteousness than by pious devotion (especially chapter 58). One magnificent section, it has been suggested, is even put into the mouth of the outcast Samaritans (chapter 63, verses 7 to 19) — "doubtless thou art our father, though Abraham be ignorant of us".

It is no wonder that these astonishing ideas proved so hard of acceptance. After all, we have had them before us now for more than 2,500 years, yet we still suppose, first, that salvation is strictly limited to a chosen few, and second, that success is one of the marks of divine favour. "I'm sure I've done nothing to deserve this," we say indignantly, when we're asked to bear a little suffering. And we suppose that the Church, which we call so often "the Body of Christ", will certainly not be treated as his human body was treated. We expect it to be well endowed (Christian Stewardship), highly respected, properly protected by law. We like to hear it speak on the radio or in the press "with authority", and we come down like anything on anyone who publicly criticises it. To persecute it openly is practically to invite a declaration of war. Messiah, so far as we are concerned, is still a king, who comes in dignity and expects proper and regal treatment. Who, indeed, hath believed the prophet's report? To whom is the true Messiah revealed?

75

DOING WHAT YOU HATE— BECAUSE YOU MUST

THE OPENING CHAPTER OF Jeremiah is full of meat. Its very first verses are a model of how a book should begin. It tells us something of the author — a parson's son — of the time at which he spoke and wrote, and of the purpose of that speaking and writing.

Prophets, as we are constantly reminded, were people whose job was to pronounce moral judgement, not to give inside information as to the future. They told their hearers what was likely to happen if they went on behaving in the way they were doing; they intended to teach rather than to forecast.

"Visual aids" are today recognised as invaluable, if lessons are to be learned effectively. The prophets, as a group, were perfectly aware of this. They were, indeed, expert in the use of such methods. The last part of our present passage illustrates two ways in which they used them. In the first, they observed some normal natural event and took it as an example. In verse 11, for instance, the blossoming sprig of an almond tree becomes a symbol of the irresistible movement of the will of God. As the sap leaps up the trunk, as the tender leaflet has the strength to crack open the paving slab, so the purpose of God works out its way. Similarly, in verse 13, a pot about to boil over provides a simile — which has passed into popular use — of imminent warfare.

The second form of "visual aid" is expressed in the deliberate dramatic gesture. At the beginning of chapter 13, for instance, the prophet is told to make use of the normal process of decay to express the breakdown of national morale; in chapter 19 the shattering of an earthen jar symbolises the breaking of the nation. Any reading of the prophetic books will produce scores of such examples. Now this is a technique which today finds its parallels in the teaching profession rather than in the Church. No one has really discovered, for instance, how religion can be made visually dramatic, in spite of all our efforts with films, drama, and T.V. But we have surely lost something through over-intellectualising, and through supposing that truth is communicated through abstract ideas without regard to concrete expression of them.

This same chapter has another point of interest. How are prophets made or discovered? Are they, for example, people born with a chip on the shoulder who find their own self-fulfilment in being the odd man out? We all know people like this. If others admire the book — they condemn it. The play they can't bear to see is the one everybody else is going to. They know the inside story of every great man, and it usually is disreputable, always discreditable. But Jeremiah wasn't at all that sort of person. He was by nature shy, anxious to be popular, frightened of the crowd. Yet the mysterious will of God has chosen him for a lonely and unattractive job, which will involve him even in charges of political treachery. And in the working out of the same mysterious will, his very weakness becomes his strength. For one thing, even at the worst, he will never totally lack friends. For another, the bitterness of his own suffering will always make him understanding and sympathetic towards the under-dog.

A tougher man might almost have enjoyed his Cassandra-role; Jeremiah hated it. He wanted just to be ordinary, raising a family like other men, leaving it to government to concern itself with state affairs and to the Church to look after God's interests. Instead, he is to bear almost alone the weight of his fore-knowledge, to show in his person some anticipation of the work of Messiah himself. For it was just because of this lonely separation, that his inner eye was opened, and, that in chapter 23, verses 3 to 8, he comes to the assurance of a new covenant, or to give it a more familiar translation, of a "New Testament". Thrust out from the country of his people, utterly alone with his God, he perceives that the New Israel will one day be united in a new Law and a new nationhood. This common bond will be the forgiveness of God : their common expression — love towards him.

It is such passages as these that help us to understand the identity of Jeremiah's life and of his message. Solitude and rejection opened his eyes, to discover that his solitude was shared and that he whom the builders rejected, the same was made the headstone of the corner. The very gifts which were his sorrow proved at last the source of his truest blessing.

76

PROPHET IN A HOLE

THIS IS A FASCINATING STORY OF what happens to journalists who spread alarm and despondency in time of war. Jeremiah has openly been encouraging disaffection — like a C.N.D. recruit active in the armed forces. His country is fighting a desperate war for survival — and he has been urging its people to save their lives by surrender.

Very naturally, then, the War Cabinet decide to silence him for good, by dropping him down an old well (not exactly a dry one, but filled with mud rather than water). In this way he would starve to death, but no one would be guilty of actually murdering him. One can imagine them shouting down from the top, *"Now* try running away from that lot."

A black man, a slave in attendance on the royal harem, comes to his rescue, gets the king's authority to plan a rescue and carries it out. In return, the desperate king begs for encouragement in the nation's war effort, but doesn't get it. He is scared of his own people and dares not suggest to them the possibility of a peace-treaty, but at least he has the strength of mind to leave Jeremiah safely in the barracks of the palace guard until the city has been taken.

This is the story of three men, two strong and one weak. How many of the disasters of history have arisen from weakness rather than strength, from the obstinacy of the small-minded who lack the courage to change a wrong policy whilst there still is time to do so? At the same time let us honestly admit that we all admire heroic, even if hopeless, endurance in defence much more than we do swift capitulation. This is partly because we see it too often from the point of view of the leader and combatant rather than from that of the underdog civilian. It may be fine for the general to order resistance to the last man : rather too often the general himself seems to *be* the last man. To be stubborn in the wrong cause is never a mark of virtue, least of all when it involves other people in suffering for a cause about which they are unenthusiastic. But it is largely when it is in desperate straits that real democracy proves its quality. For true democracy really does arouse a genuine and universal strength to resist and courage to endure, so that a people will resist "on the beaches, in the fields, in the hills". Tyranny can only order a scorched-earth policy, which its minions take very good care not to implement. What we have to decide for ourselves in each instance is whether the will to resist is morally justified or whether it is the mark of a higher courage and a deeper sense of duty to urge surrender.

With King Zedekiah, compare the Ethiopian Ebed-melech. In the first place, he dares to identify himself with a thoroughly unpopular figure, and to do it, not only by word, but by deed. A whisper in the king's ear on an unnoticed occasion would have been enough for most of us to risk, but no, he goes openly with a squad to defy the Cabinet's order. Further, a man of compassion and imagination, he realises how the rope will cut into the emaciated body of a starving man gripped tight in stinking slime. He improvises a kind of life-belt to take the strain.

Over and again history mentions, just in passing, the names or persons of those who come to the aid of great ones in their troubles. Whether it be Blondel the minstrel seeking out Coeur de Lion; Flora Macdonald sheltering Bonnie Prince Charlie; the heroic householders of Europe who risked — and gave — their lives for partisan and escapee, the unwritten records are full of such instances, though often only recorded in the grateful memories of those directly concerned. Few of us may have the courage or the opportunity to stand like Jeremiah, alone against the total tide of popular opinion. But to most of us comes some opportunity of showing a little kindness to an outcast, and of defying the verdict of society by coming to the help of its victims. Ebed-melech didn't necessarily share the opinions of Jeremiah : indeed, he may have thought them abominable. But he wasn't going to let a fellow-creature die in mud and darkness for want of courage on his own part. He is not the least of the many Africans whose names shine out amongst the lesser heroes of the Bible record, a record which includes an Ethiopian Minister of State (Acts, chapter 8, verse 27), along with Simon of Cyrene, who carried the very cross of Christ.

77

THE GLOOM OF JEREMIAH

THERE IS ONE VERSE IN THIS neglected book that we all know from innumerable Good Friday posters — chapter 1, verse 12. It is generally used, of course, quite out of context, just because it provides a moving commentary on the passion of Christ. But in itself it summarises the theme of the whole book — the tragedy of fallen Jerusalem, so touchingly described in this last chapter.

This gives an account of a people enslaved, who must buy from others the fruits of their own land (verse 4), begging in the street from foreigners (verse 6), searching desperately for food in the desert (verse 9), seeing their children staggering under burdens (verse 13). Because, greatest disaster of all, Mount Zion, home of the living God, is now the home of jackals (verse 18).

It is always tempting to blame present failure or past misfortune, and to excuse personal or national inability to cope with our problems, on the ground that we have never really had a chance. This is the reverse side of that false pride which expects present admiration for past performance. Too many of our public festivities and attitudes reflect one of these alternatives. There really seems at this date as little cause for the English to be pleased at Guy Fawkes' failure as for the Irish to be bitter over Cromwell's success.

Now, Jewish history, as we have seen (Exodus 12), until the capture of Jerusalem in 586 B.C., balanced upon a pivotal occasion — the delivery from Egypt. This was the date celebrated both in the Passover Feast and in the stories and songs of the people to which all else looked back. It was the proof, underlined though this was on many subsequent occasions, that they were God's people indeed, and that he would always deliver them in their need.

But this balance was gravely upset when the holy city was visibly overthrown. Politically, the reason for this destruction were fairly obvious. Palestine stands straddling the coast road from Egypt in the south-west to the "Fertile Crescent" between the Tigris and Euphrates rivers to the north-east. Whenever these two groups of powers wanted to invade each other it was through Palestine they must pass. Samaria and the Northern Kingdom were mopped up first: Jerusalem in its hills — "like a bird in its cage" as a contemporary describes it — could only hold out either by a scrupulous and Swiss neutrality (which was usually impossible anyway) or by managing to emerge on the winning side. For a time this proved possible; but at last, in the reign of King Zedekiah and the year 586 B.C., the end came, the city was sacked, and the greater part of its population carried away. It says a great deal for the vitality and sense of Judaism that an event so shattering did not, in fact, shatter; their morale, as the later (in date) books of the Old Testament tell us, revived, and the city was rebuilt. But the blow was a fearful one, and it left a scar behind it. They had been so certain that God would never allow his holy city to be taken, that he *must* intervene if it were seriously threatened — as so often, they believed, he had intervened before. Political reasons could surely never outweigh the protection of God?

We all have, of course, our Jerusalems. We all have certain areas of experience, of prejudices and of practice, which we cannot imagine can ever cease to survive.

We see it over social and moral matters, where we tend to regard a tradition we endorse as the unchangeable law of God. We see it very clearly in the ecclesiastical world, where every faith and every denomination has its private Jerusalem, whether it be called the Principles of the Reformation, True Catholic Practice, or the Thirty-Nine Articles. We see it in politics, and in the absolute certainty with which Western democracy is equated with the will of God. What we must learn, as, for example, the Church in China and East Germany have had to

158

learn, is that God is not limited to whatever Jerusalem we build for him, and that when his temple is destroyed, he is still to be found in the homes and hearts of his friends. We must always be on our guard against all and any identification of the eternal with the temporal, and against supposing that the world ends when our corner of it is disturbed. Life goes on, even when an applecart is upset — hard though the apples may find this to believe.

78

WHEELS WITHIN WHEELS

EZEKIEL WAS A PARSON BY calling, and as the priesthood went by descent among the Jews this meant that he was also a parson's son, brought up in the neighbourhood of the temple. Carried away with the captives from Jerusalem to Babylonia in 597 B.C., at the age of twenty-five, he found himself called to a thoroughly unpopular job. He was to tell his people that the tale of disaster was not yet finished, and that there was to be no easy deliverance for them.

In the year 586 they saw his words come true; the city of Jerusalem was completely destroyed, and the temple burnt to the ground.

Now the revelations of truth granted to him came in the form of visions. In these visions sometimes he saw supernatural beings, sometimes he was shown ordinary human affairs. But both kinds of vision had a quality of "in-sight", of making plain the inside meaning of situations normally only seen from the outside.

Thus, when he looks at supernatural beings he sees represented *visibly* in them the qualities which they personify — rather as in a cartoon we show "greed" with a pig's head, or "speed" with wings on his heels. We are to think of these beings as impersonating these qualities completely, as being a quality made absolute and real.

In this first chapter, for instance, he sees certain divine creatures, symbolic heavenly beings, which represent in themselves a whole range of splendour.

For one thing, they have the power of being omnipresent, a speed greater than light itself, so that they can be, at one and the same moment, both here and also there. This is symbolised in their wheels and in their wings. One commentator, indeed, has suggested that they are really exercises in solid geometry, animated mathematical symbols! Indeed, why not? Is not God interested in mathematics?

Again, they have too the power of "total awareness", symbolised by the eyes on every side of them, and the fact that they move in every direction without turning their regard. They glow with unquenchable brightness, and the sound of them is the diapason of nature itself. For these beings do indeed represent Nature, but Nature as it should be, totally obedient to God.

This is why one of them resembles a man — but represents mankind glorified. Another resembles an ox — and in that ox are all domestic animals fulfilled. Another is like a lion, in which the ultimate magnificence of wild nature becomes fully and finally itself as it was meant to be. The fourth is an eagle, the bird which, so men believed, could soar from earth into heaven. These beings remind us that both the creatures of this world and the inhabitants of worlds beyond are known all of them as children of the same God. He is "maker of all things, visible and invisible".

From the very start of the book, therefore, we know that we are going to be allowed to share this inside view of the situation. Sometimes, no doubt, this will be very puzzling. If you travel beyond dimensions of space and time, you find them awkward and limited when you look back into and through them. Sometimes, too, we shall be brought back with a bump to the human situation in which the prophet is working, and shown the fear and hostility which his visions naturally arouse. No one *likes* to be reminded that he is purblind, and, sweet though the message may be to the man who receives it from God (as at the beginning of chapter 3), it is undeniably bitter when it is passed on to the people for whom it is intended and illustrated with suitable visual aids.

The first twenty-four chapters of the book maintain this theme and that of judgement for past sin. Now we may feel that all this talk of "idol-worship" and "false gods" has little enough to do with us. But we can put it in another way. A god is what you worship, that to which you attribute worth and importance. Ezekiel is simply saying that if a nation gets its source of values wrong, if it puts first things last, it will quite certainly involve itself in trouble. Wrong choice of action is called "sin". Sin is called "deadly" because it's a killer. Natural wrong choice, then, brings natural death — whether at the hands of Babylonia or of any other contemporary enemy.

79

THE RATS IN THE WAINSCOT

OF ALL THE MAJOR BOOKS OF THE Old Testament, the prophet Ezekiel is perhaps the hardest to enjoy (with the sole exception of Leviticus). He writes for his own people, now captive in Babylon, in order to explain why they are suffering so bitterly in the present, and how, in time to come, their sufferings will be turned to joy. A good parallel to his work can be found in Psalm 137, with its mixture of wistful recollection, dedication to the continuance of the national dream, and furious hatred for those who have brought about the situation.

The book has a structure and a theme. It begins with the revelation of God's message to Ezekiel in the river plain of his exile, and it analyses the failure of the Israelites to appreciate God's judgement, even when it falls upon their neighbours. It ends in a dream of the New Jerusalem, a picture so remote as to be almost out of this earth, but a city so affectionately described in its detail as to be a kind of preliminary draft of the vision of St. John.

Ezekiel was himself a priest, and there are moments when he gets so excited at the thought of planning the services of the new

L

temple and of organising the morals of its worshippers, as to move altogether out of the world of lay concern into that of the ecclesiastical outfitter.

But there are moments too when his vision suddenly focusses, and then the picture is often as brilliant as a colour-transparency.

Chapter 8 is such a vision. He is sitting in his house, enjoying the company of his respectable friends, when he goes into a trance. In that trance a dazzling angelic figure carries him away and puts him down in Jerusalem, opposite the temple itself. Here he discovers corruption. This, the very heart of the faith, is already riddled with the shapes of idolatry.

There are four of these. The first (verse 3) is the "image of jealousy". This is possibly that "queen of heaven" whom women worshipped (Jeremiah 44, verses 15 to 19). She represents then the goddess who is invoked to secure the return of a straying lover, or to bring about the death of a rival for his affections. The second is a secret underground collection of monstrous animals — such as were worshipped in Egypt, the cat, the jackal, and the crocodile. These are the personification of man's animal attributes, the totem figures of tribal religion. The third embodies the cult of Adonis, the beautiful young man slain by a boar and mourned for ever by his unhappy mother. He figures in Greek as well as Levantine mythology. And the fourth group are the sun worshippers, who turn their backs on the temple for the purpose.

Now this is not the only passage in which Ezekiel attacks in detail idolatrous corruptions; chapter 13, verses 17 to 19, for instance, refers to the "soul-catchers", the ill-wishers who cause people to pine and die. But most of his condemnation is in general terms, and directed not so much against the idols themselves as against the disloyalty which led the two kingdoms of Israel and Judah to worship them.

What are the deep human instincts expressed within the religious corruptions of this particular section? They seem to stand for four traditions constant in religious history, nor is it difficult to find four modern perversions of faith which seem to relate to the four described by Ezekiel.

"An image which provokes to jealousy" — that is familiar

enough. For many of us our brand-image of the Church is something to be jealously watched and anxiously protected. Any suggestion of criticism from within or without is to be resented and condemned. Questionings from within are treachery and heresy: comments from without are uninformed and therefore to be disregarded. The Church is the Church as we know and like it; any other suggestion is perversion. We will only have reunion by allowing others to join us; we will only approach the world to the extent of allowing it to come in on our terms. This image squats guarding the approach to our temple — and it is very difficult to get past it.

Others of us are like the Rev. J. Shaphanson and his friends (see verse 11 of this chapter). We have turned our backs on reality, and buried ourselves away from the world. Even the subjects of our worship are at second-hand, pictures rather than realities, images and projections of a life which is remote from us. So we busy ourselves with details of ecclesiastical lingerie, and the very air we breathe is tainted with the smell of pseudo-sanctity. We become church-parasites, spending our time in conference, guild and association, all devoted to purposes which seem to the outsider as absorbing, doubtless, but also as significant as a collection of eighteenth-century snuff-boxes. Even to reach us in our murky retreat means determined digging.

Others find their satisfaction in weeping for Thammuz. These are the wallowers in emotion, the easy weepers, the people whose loyalty is to dear Father So-and-so and the sweet little church where he ministers — or alternatively, to the revival services which they attend for the purpose of reconversion. Religion to them is a "lovely cry"; and where their emotions lead them, thither they will go — for good or bad. Generous if their hearts are touched by a suitable sermon, they are hard as concrete in other connexions.

Finally, the sun-worshippers. If there is one thing which is absolutely certain, it is that the sun represents a totally impersonal deity. Nothing we can say or do influences his course — nor can we even pretend, as we do with the stars and planets, that his movements influence ours. Yet he is, in his way, a highly effective deity. He quite obviously is *useful*.

163

The sun-worshipper's parallel today is, perhaps, the man who thinks a moral code is a good thing for people to have and is all in favour of the Establishment. His god is deliberately impersonal, an amalgam of recollections of his nanny, his schoolmaster, and the social pressures which have moulded him. He does not expect his God to do anything outside his expected behaviour-pattern, and so long as he sticks to this, his worshipper will stick to him. This is the type of upright man who made the Pharisee long ago — and makes him still. Then, as now, it was his particular tragedy that by turning his back on the living truth he rejects the very possibility of change.

EZEKIEL 37. 1–14

80

SKELETON ARMY

IT IS RATHER STRANGE THAT WE should use a skeleton as the symbol of death, whether as the skull and crossbones of the pirate or the bony dance of death which so appealed to the mediaeval mind.

Death is to us the evidence of impermanence — the clear proof that everything passes away. Yet it is the flesh and sinew which change and decay, whereas it is the bone structure alone which survives even for centuries. The skeleton, then, might well represent survival and immortality.

But, perhaps our attitude looks back to the Jewish identification of life with blood (with all the "Kosher" regulations as to slaughtering animals that have arisen from this identification). The life must be totally quit, the blood gone, before the meat can be eaten, or else we are guilty of devouring life itself. If blood, the warm, the moving, represents life, then bleached bones may well stand for death. Golgotha, place of death, is the hill of the skull. The picture therefore that Ezekiel paints is a picture of total death. Not only does he see a charnel-place of bones, like the legendary elephants' burying-ground, but they

164

are a chaos of scattered, unidentified bones, dry with the dust of ages, most dreadfully dead. Into this dusty desolation a wind begins to blow. Over and over again in the Bible this wind is the sign of God's living presence, the breath of his life and the breath that gives life. As it whispers above them, so the bones begin to stir, to take shape, to take *individual* shapes. And as they resume their own proper form and relationship, so, like leafless trees in spring, they begin to bud and blossom into flesh. They *live* again, no longer arid confusion, but a host of separate men.

Ezekiel gave this as a clear-cut illustration of the ability of God to revive a dead nation, and to revive it in terms of the individual human beings of whom it is made.

Now there is nothing so difficult as to *recreate* something which has died. If we think of a nation with a mighty past and a distressing present (and it is easy to think of such), or a football team that has sunk from the top of the First Division to the bottom of the Third, or a parish that has fallen on evil days, or a society that has lost its purpose — we know how rare and difficult an achievement is a true "come-back". It is usually much easier to start afresh with a new set-up. Yet here, says the prophet, is an ultimate and total deadness, the deadness of the moon or of an extinguished fire. And here, he says, is a new kind of life gently breathed into and over the cadaver, a power that can overcome death itself.

We can find parallels in our own experience. It may be an organisation we are asked to take on: it may be a seemingly hopeless family situation: it may be a business to be nursed back to life. But if the job is meant for us, and we believe the effort is meant to be made, then this story suggests that there can be no state of utter hopelessness, no problem beyond solution, no bones so dead that they cannot live again. Our problem may well be to decide whether or not this particular skeleton is meant for burial or revival: there is a kind of puppet-dance in which the bones move in a semblance of life as we jerk the strings by which they are suspended. But when we are sure that the dead are indeed called to live again then we may wait for the wind to blow with a sense of certain expectation, and with, sometimes, a patient sorting-out of the bones until it does blow. Revival is of God, but this does not excuse man from any duties either of anticipation or of collaboration. The wind bloweth where it listeth — but it blows, too, in response to prayer and expectation.

DANIEL
(summary)

81

DREAMS AND THEIR MEANING

To PRIMITIVE MAN, DREAMS ARE important, because they are his evidence for life after death. In sleep, the body lies still — but some interior self of the sleeper is well aware of the experiences, good or bad, through which he seems to be passing. Death looks like a sleep, even if it be an unbroken one. May not the dead man, therefore, be dreaming? May there not be some unknown world in which his dreaming self continues to live and to experience? So he makes practical preparation for this new world either by including in the grave-space food and weapons, valuables and domestic animals which will dream with their owner, or also by "mummying" the body to preserve it against the day when the returning soul will need it, as it awakens from its dream of death and takes up the business of life.

But if dreams are our anticipation of life after death, then presumably they are also a form of communication with it, and of the beings who already exist within it? Again, evidence seemed clear. In dreams men met again the parents or friends they had known and loved in life. How natural, then, to receive messages through dreams, direct commands, warnings or encouragement!

Moreover, since that other world is outside our limitations of time and space — limitations of which almost every dream makes nonsense — then it is natural to suppose that we may, in these dream messages, anticipate the future?

And how natural that those who believed in one supreme and omnipotent God should suppose that he would use this same channel of communication. The Greeks, rational and hard-headed as they were, believed firmly in this and appointed certain temples as centres of such dream divination.

How does this affect us? A hundred years ago we laughed at dreams and talked of "toasted-cheese nightmares".

But today two new forms of knowledge have compelled us to take dreams seriously. The first, the more speculative, is linked with "extra-sensory perception", and that mysterious and so far indefinable ability of certain persons, in certain circumstances, to foretell such simple events in time as the fall of a card. Perhaps the best-known book in this field is Dunne's *Experiment with Time*. Briefly, he suggests that each of us contains a whole range of selves, some of whom only communicate with us in sleep, when the surface-selves are quiet. But the communication may be important, revealing to us truth which we are disregarding. And some of the selves, he suggests, operate outside space and time and can therefore "remember" the future as easily as the past.

The second form of knowledge has been opened to us through the work of the psycho-analysts. They have stressed the importance of the hidden self, the subconscious, whose messages to us are converted by a faculty in us which, as it were, *codes* the message and presents it in a form our conscious self can disregard as irrelevant and nonsensical. But it is often an immensely important message, revealing to us our repressed desires, our secret fears and hates. We need to understand these, if we are to come to terms with them and cope with them effectively.

But first of all, we have to learn the secret language through which the subconscious communicates. Few of us take the trouble or discover the technique. And this is why dreams have always needed an interpreter, whether he be the Harley Street expert or a Hebrew prophet. Each of those interpreters recognises the dream as a channel through which unsuspected truth is being conveyed, whether this refer to external events anticipated, or to inner disposition (and so future potential) revealed. The dream, then, is — or can be — the mode of communication of our deepest self, as it tries to make itself known to our surface and conscious self. Yet the conscious self has the power to distort as well as to reject. It can shut its eyes and ears to the truth presented. The God within speaks — but we can disregard the whisper or assume it is in a foreign tongue and mere gibberish at that.

DANIEL 6

82

OUT OF THE MOUTHS OF LIONS

THE BOOK OF DANIEL HAS TWO themes, which are really one and the same. God, it maintains, does not desert those who trust in him, whether they be individuals (half the book is concerned with these) or nations (the theme of the other half).

The stories about nations are written in a kind of picture-language, in which the prophet comments upon world-affairs as though he were anticipating history and detecting the trends within it (just as in the New Testament, the Christians so often look *back* into history with the same idea of analysing its direction and separating its contributing causes).

The stories about individuals are direct narratives, which can be compared with, say, the ballads of Charlemagne, the heroic legends of Brasidas and Horatius, or the stories which accumulate round every great general even in living experience. Are they literally true? Impossible to tell. Are they based on truth? Certainly, but a truth which has been handed on, varied, and embellished, till no one may dare to deny it or hope to analyse it.

Now this particular story has about it a real feeling of personality. Both Daniel and Darius do seem to be people, and not just symbols or puppets.

This is particularly true of Darius. He has caused savage jealousy by appointing a foreigner as his Grand Vizier (the Joseph situation all over again). He is induced to sign a decree drafted by Daniel's envious rivals. He finds out that he has been tricked, and does all he can to help his friend and loyal servant. When human efforts fail, he hopes that Daniel's God may prove more effective. He mourns for his friend's fate, is delighted at his salvation, and takes effective action to see that the situation will not recur.

It is important to remember that his one real mistake was in signing the decree without proper thought. He did what so many of us do, whether in H.P., a lease or insurance policy — or even in writing an ill-advised letter; he committed himself without seeing what the consequences would be. Having so committed himself, he could not rightly withdraw. As we saw in the story of Jephthah that oaths *must* be kept if there is to be a moral base within society, so laws must be maintained even when they bear down on the individual. "Hard cases make bad law." If the king had demanded the right to cancel a law once ratified, or his great vizier had been treated as exempt from it, the very nature of Law would have been attacked.

This the king could not do, and Daniel evidently agreed. He may well have felt, however, that if only Darius had had the sense to discuss the bill with his Prime Minister before giving it royal assent a great deal of trouble would have been saved. As it was, an apparently venal fault, a mere lack of thought, very nearly destroyed an innocent man.

Now on Daniel's side we begin with a magnificent tribute paid to him by his enemies. They search for a stick to beat him, and admit that he has no weakness they can exploit.

He can't be bribed or intimidated, he has no dubious sexual relationships, he doesn't fill the state department with his kith and kin or his cronies — in fact, he has no Achilles' heel at all. So they resolve to attack him over his faith. They see that he makes his god and his conscience supreme : through these they will destroy him. (Note that had the king been more alert they would not have succeeded : this is the Lear-Cordelia situation when folly must intervene if innocence is to be condemned.)

And Daniel replies to their plot with splendid defiance. No creeping off to the cellar for silent devotions, no compromising with public opinion until the thirty days are up and better times begun. He opens his windows wide, and prays unashamedly and aloud. He won't weather this storm by shortening sail : he holds his course direct into the heart of it. This may be bad seamanship, but there are times when it is true Christianity. Yet, to be fair, we must also agree that there are times, as in the case of Naaman and the House of Rimmon, when compromise also is right. The problem for the Christian is to see what may be his proper course in the situation in which he finds himself, rather than to look for an absolute and universal rule-of-thumb. Nor yet are we to use this stirring story as evidence that God *always* delivers those who trust in him. Daniel was delivered from the lions : thousands of Christian martyrs in the arena were not. Yet God was no less concerned with them than with him. The "happy" ending lies not in the fact that "they lived happy ever after" as in the integrity and courage with which the situation is faced.

83

THE DYNASTS

THIS IS AN EXTRAORDINARY chapter, in which the nation-states of the known world are identified with supernatural individuals. It seems to be a transition from the belief we have found elsewhere in the Old Testament — that each nation has its own God who champions it in war — to the later concept of personal guardian-angels. In each case there is recognition of some affinity between the worlds visible and invisible; above all, that the supernatural is concerned with the natural, and is active in its affairs.

The story begins with Daniel preparing for his vision by fasting. That a low diet does improve powers of perception and intuition is a piece of knowledge common to all religions. It is even endorsed by those current financiers and politicians who, at huge cost, return to remote nursing homes to live on orange juice and cold water.

Eventually the vision takes place — not, it is interesting to see, when Daniel is alone, though the persons with him (like those with Saul on the Damascus road) experience only fear without revelation.

First comes the appearance — in the shape of a being of human likeness, yet dazzling luminosity, so awe-inspiring that the seer falls into a dead faint. He is aroused from it by a touch, which persuades him to rise as far as his hands and knees. But God does not ask for servility. He must stand up like a man and hold conversation with the messenger. So, one by one, he recovers his senses — sight, hearing, speech, understanding. He is, stage by stage, given the strength he needs to sustain contact with the tremendous reality of the spiritual world, in comparison with which the material one is only a tenuous shadow.

This, surely, is the point of the vision. We are accustomed to think of our world of knowledge and affairs as the real one, where decisions are taken and futures decided. But Daniel offers us instead a picture of "Principalities and Powers", beings, good and bad, who resemble the nation-representatives to be seen in old *Punch* cartoons, where "John Bull" stands for England, "Uncle Sam" for America, and a shaggy bear for Russia. In the vision, these representatives maintain their country's rights before the heavenly throne, as ambassadors do before an earthly government. Michael, the great archangel, lends the weight of his authority to the cause of Israel (sponsored, in the first place, by the shining man of vision). But Persia "withstands" him (Persia had now become Israel's overlord) and in due course will be succeeded by Greece (as Alexander and the Seleucid kings overthrow the Persian empire).

We shall be plunged, in the next chapters, into an analysis of Israelite history, in which most of the characters can be identified from our knowledge of events. Attempts have been made, of course, to abstract this analysis from its contemporary reference, and to make it refer to subsequent world history. Oliver Cromwell, Napoleon, the Kaiser, Stalin — all these have been detected, and doubtless until the end of time pseudo-students will continue to discover appropriate resemblances to their own day.

171

There seems, however, very little possible doubt that these passages were written, either with hindsight in reflexion upon the past, or as a contemporary judgement, in order to cheer the hearts of the faithful. Just as God stood by the "Three Children" in the fiery furnace, so he stands by his people within the historical situation.

His use of these "Dynast" beings allows the writer an explanation of why it is that nations rise and fall — sometimes, it would seem, without moral justification. How, men ask, can God permit cruel and depraved peoples to defeat and massacre their neighbours? Because, Daniel replies, nations, like men, are entities. They have freedom allowed them for good or evil — yet they too stand under judgement. In earlier passages of the book the "entity" or "identity" of the nation is concentrated in one man, its ruler. We are shown these rulers, Nebuchadnezzar and Belshazzar, sentenced by divine justice, in one case to a term of "preventive detention" and in the second, to death. But now the idea is extended. The symbolic figure rises from earth to heaven. It is no longer the king earthly, but the prince heavenly who represents the people, and — as verse 21 rather wistfully notes — in heaven as on earth the great powers are still ganging up against Israel.

84

THE BETRAYAL OF LOVE

THERE ARE TWO FORMS OF morality — Law and Righteousness. In an ideal situation, the two coincide, so that conscience reinforces legislation, and the state expresses in legal pattern that which all its members believe to be right. In practice, the divergence is considerable and sometimes deliberate. The law, like a convoy, tends to move at the speed of its slowest adherent.

And there are two kinds of human relationship, that of *Choice* and that of *Contract* or *Status*. Here again, ideally, these two are one, so that we "love" those with whom we are associated. Sometimes it breaks down. We discover that we dislike our blood-relations, that we cannot get along with husband or wife, that we distrust our employer or envy our fellow-workers. What then are we to do about it? The Book of Hosea attempts to answer this, before Christ came to give an answer more complete.

It shows God in the position of one who loves, and is betrayed, rather than as one who commands and is disobeyed, or one who makes a covenant-bargain, which is broken.

In this particular passage, it is the love of a father which is disappointed. A father who teaches his little son to walk, who carries him in his arms, feeds and comforts him. The child rejects his father and stubbornly pursues his own disastrous way. In verses 5 to 7 the father's anger blazes up — but by verse 8 he is again thinking in terms of love and forgiveness to his own flesh and blood and by verse 11 the prodigal son is already returning home.

The last chapter — 14 — is simply a reassertion of the eternal forgiving mercy of God most nobly expressed.

Now this theme of forgiving love was most strangely and terribly experienced in Hosea's own life. Looking out at the way both kingdoms of Judah and Israel had rejected God, he felt called to marry a woman of easy virtue — or, it may be, the wife in whom he had trusted turned out to be such a one. But buy her he did, to keep her from her trade (chapter 3, verses 1 to 3), and betray him she did, it seems, thereafter.

Incidentally, Hosea was, it is supposed, by occupation a baker (chapter 7, verses 4 to 8), unlike the statesmen and farmers from whom others of the lay-prophets were drawn.

The situation behind the story is of course an old and familiar one. What is the right way to treat the deviant partner in a relationship? Is it enough just to condone, to accept whatever is done, to go on loving and waiting and hoping? Is there a stage at which the offence against love is so heinous that it is better to cut one's losses and try again? Or is Hosea right, and is the way of God the way man must try to follow, whether or no it succeeds in any human sense? What is clear and is important is that we need not think of Hosea as deliberately selecting a worthless woman just to point the moral : we may equally well see in him a man who finds comfort, in his own marriage problems, in the thought that God too knows what it is to find love rejected and trust outraged.

85

LOCUSTS ON THE MARCH

ANGLICANS OF THE CURRENT "Parish Communion" tradition hear very little of the Old Testament, to their own serious loss. But there are one or two mornings when, in place of the Epistle, they get a "Lection" from the prophets. Ash Wednesday is one of these, with its passage from Joel (chapter 2, verses 12 to 17). The same chapter, from verse 28 to the end, was quoted by St. Peter on the first Whitsunday — which is why we have taken the whole chapter to typify the prophet and his thought.

His theme is a clear-cut one. There has been an appalling locust plague, along with a drought. Chapter 1, verses 16 to 20 describes a scene dreadfully convincing to farmers from warmer lands — soil as hard as concrete, wretched herds mooing miserably as they drift in hopeless search of water or pasture, barns empty and derelict. Chapter 2 begins with the locust armies on the march and goes on to call people to penitence, to a national day of prayer for the whole nation. The response is instant. High winds drive off the insect plagues, the land blooms again with plenty, and a grateful people respond not only with praise but in new powers of the Spirit.

In chapter 3 doom is pronounced upon the seaboard nations who have been selling the boys and girls of Israel into slavery. Here we find anticipated the thought of Armageddon, the great battle-at-the-end-of-the-world which also occurs in Norse mythology. Armageddon is just Har-Megiddo (= "the valley of Megiddo"), that highway between desert and sea where so many of the fiercest battles of Palestinian history were fought. After this battle, Israel will be established for ever, with God dwelling in his holy city of Jerusalem in the midst of it.

Unlike many of his brother-prophets, Joel sees no particular *reason* for the divine anger expressed in drought and famine. The prayer to which he calls people is anguished entreaty for survival, not penitence for any specific sins. What do we think of this attitude to disasters in the natural sphere? Do we, for instance, believe in praying for rain or — more probably, in this country — fine weather? Here we have to face a real problem. The Gospels state quite clearly that winds and waves obey Christ, and that at his death the whole natural world responded with earthquake and darkness. They accept what is called in poets "the Pathetic Fallacy", the idea that nature expresses emotions which endorse our own, that rain "weeps", and sunshine "smiles", stormclouds "lour" and snow "mercifully conceals". It is then perfectly sensible to pray that God will work upon the will of these daemonic powers, as we pray him to turn the hearts of our enemies.

But do we really believe that nature *is* like that? Are high and low pressure areas affected by our needs or our prayers? Are droughts or floods the result of divine anger, and can they therefore be voided through our penitence? Should our children be encouraged to pray for sunshine for the picnic, or do we prefer the attitude of the incumbent who refused to use the set prayers for fair weather whilst the barometer remained so low? Or is there another possibility? Is the really important object of our prayer our own attitude in the face of the weather? So that we shall be patient and enduring in the bad, and grateful and appreciative of good? So that we shall not expect everything to suit our own convenience, but ask for help to meet the situation whatever it may be?

Along with this, however — and illogical as it may seem in our most rational moments — there often goes a deeper sense in which we are not ashamed or afraid to communicate to our Father our desires and hopes, however trivial — and can we presume to say that he does not sometimes intervene to grant them? Love is not always strictly logical. Surely then, we may

pour out our needs before God, in the certainty that our prayer
will be answered. But the answer will not always or necessarily
take the shape of visible mercy: it may come instead as invisible
strength.

Amos 5. 6–24

86

PEAKED FACES OF THE PEASANTS

Russia in the nineteenth
century contained two potential parties of revolution. One looked
to the peasant as the fuel of the fire that would come, and to
the *"Mir"*, the landed commune, as the unit of the new Russia.
The other, which won out in the end, accepted Marxism as its
gospel and the development of an industrial proletariat as its
aim. But there was a time when it looked as though it would be
the peasants who finally kicked over the cauldron of the social
order — as it was peasants who marched on Versailles in 1789,
and on London in 1381.

For the peasant is all too clearly confronted — as the industrial worker is not — with the disproportion between his work
and its result. He produces the food and the clothing that others
will enjoy. He lives on the frontier of starvation — and he can
see food all round him. The industrial worker, on the other
hand — at least until the development of cheap mass-com-
munications — was one of a crowd of others like him, whose
labour appeared quite dispensable, whose particular contribution
to an end-product seemed negligible. He learned solidarity and
fellowship, because these were the only possible channels of expression open to him.

Amos is the book of a revolutionary peasant, and resembles
in this the poetry of Piers Plowman. A shepherd, looking down
from his mountain pastures on the kingdom of his world, he
saw that world as doomed. And he saw that doom expressed in
what later generations have learned to call the *"dialectic of*

history", the process by which all events are interlocked with — and — affect each other. This is the secular expression of an idea expressed by the Christian as the "Divine Purpose".

Amos therefore begins his book with condemnation on every nation of his neighbourhood, on Syrian and Philistine, on Phoenician and Bedouin. He includes in this judgement both Judah and Israel (chapters 1 and 2). Chapter 3 is a statement about historical events, about the relations to the situations of his day, or war and famine, and then (in chapters 6, 7, and 8) reiterates the theme in dramatic imagery. With chapter 9 comes a great vision of divine wrath, including an extraordinary passage (verses 7 to 10) in which God is described as intervening in *world* history as much as in the destiny of Israel itself. It is astonishing to find this country herdsman so well aware of world-movements, so international in his thinking and concern.

Chapter 5 is perhaps the distillation of the entire book. It preaches a direct 'social religion' not only alongside but over against a formal one. There is, says Amos, no hope at all in a "faith" which is not also expressed in "works". To trust in God is not enough, unless that trust be built upon justice and mercy towards men.

It can be paraphrased something like this (verses 10 to 24): "You will not listen to truth. You have become oppressive land lords — but your estates are doomed. You corrupt justice by your wealth, and silence the voice of criticism. There's just a hope for you, if you face facts and abandon the delusion that God is on your side and everything will come out all right. But the faith you think is your strength will let you down. God detests your splendid church services. He will have nothing to do with your stewardship schemes and voluntary offerings. He cannot bear the sound of the expensive new organ, or listen to your highly-paid choir — whilst you deny men justice and abandon honesty."

This is the note of prophecy which Amos shares with Micah, a perception of the nature of God which was just as hard for his contemporaries to accept as it is hard for many of the devout of today. It is a good deal easier to worship God with our lips than to serve him with our lives.

M

87

ΤΟΟ MUCH TO SWALLOW?

THERE CAN BE NO INCIDENT IN
the whole Bible which has so much worried the literalist and
amused the atheist as the story of Jonah and the fish. For "fish"
is what the Bible calls it : it is our efforts to accommodate the
respective sizes that have turned it into a whale.

But the fish is not, of course, in any way essential to the story.
Let it be a drifting log, and the interest is just the same. It is the
fact and not the means of rescue which concerns us.

Jonah is given a job to do which he doesn't like. It involves
not only travelling to a remote and probably hostile city, but
also delivering a message which will certainly not be popular.
So he decides on escape, and plans a voyage to Tartessus (not
St. Paul's city of Tarsus, but what is now Cadiz and was then
considered the very end of the world). Yet no one can escape
his vocation. At sea it catches up with him, and Jonah knows it.
Wesley and John Newton both discovered their fate in a gale,
and so it happens to Jonah. He decides that he is guilty of the sin
of disloyalty and cowardice, and that his guilt must not involve
innocent men. He will die so that they may live.

The sailors admire courage. Once they know, as they think,
the cause of the trouble, they do their very utmost to save the
situation by seamanship. It is only when that fails that they
agree to Jonah's own proposal, and overboard he goes.

But, as with Galilee centuries later, so now with the Mediterranean, God is master of wind and wave, and Jonah comes safe
to land. Where he landed we do not know, but it was not so
remote that, when the second call came, he could not start at
once for Nineveh.

The rest of the story is better read than told. But it has its
own special significance for all those who, like Jonah, are critics
of others and percipient of faults, however rightly. It is that we
don't really *want* other people to improve, and indeed some-

times find it impossible to admit that they *have* improved. Once we've put them firmly in the category of a "wrong 'un" — for whatever reason — we do not like to hear of stories to their credit or evidence of their success. Some of those who are most active in good works for others are most reluctant to see any sign of betterment in the people they claim to help. In general, those who differ from us in attitude and opinion are not, we feel, entitled to happiness or prosperity and we are resentful when they seem to obtain these. The world, which owes us our comforts and amenities, ought certainly to deny them to those who are not as we are. Indeed, we sometimes resent *any* sharing of our advantages, since this tends to make them seem less distinguished and ourselves less important and enviable.

So much for Jonah : the whale we may forget, the worm we should remember. And those who are fond of animals may find special pleasure in the final sentence. God, it appears, has pity upon cows as well as upon human beings.

MICAH 3 ; 6. 1–8

88

JUDGEMENT ON THE CHURCH

WE HAVE NOT REFERRED TO THE various "Reformations" of the Jewish nation — reformations which consisted rather in a recall to orthodox religion than in any modification of that religion itself. Yet in fact there were a number of these.

Perhaps the most famous was that organised by King Josiah of Judah, described in detail in 2 Chronicles 34. This began (verse 14) with the accidental finding of a book — very probably a copy of the Mosaic Law — hidden in the temple to avoid the persecution of one of the idolatrous earlier reigns. It went on, in the light of what the book had to say, to the wholesale purification of public life and public worship. But this was by no means the first of such periods of religious revival : another, scarcely less drastic and effective, took place under King Hezekiah (2 Chronicles 29, 30, 31).

Yet, at the very time these reforms were in full blast, prophets of the calibre of Micah were convinced of the inner corruption of the whole spiritual and economic system they were intended to reconstruct.

This is the significant background to the sound and thunder of Micah's cadences, which fall upon the ear like the muffled beat of drums leading to the scaffold. The entire establishment he sees as rotted to the core, so that the most feverish efforts reveal fresh reason for revolution rather than hope of reform.

What is the good, Micah asks in chapter 6, of restoring worship in its most splendid forms? What is the justification of gigantic cathedral musical programmes or the most lavish of free-will offerings, if the whole relationship of people to each other is totally wrong? God is not to be bribed by the appearance of devotion when every action of the devout insults his justice. (Compare the views expressed in the Epistle of St. James.)

And who are responsible? Why, the very clergy themselves, with their "easy speeches, that comfort cruel men". Across the centuries we can read these tremendous denunciations either with appreciation — or with penitence. Have we no formulae of self-deceit, administered so glibly in the name of the Lord, so casually taking that Name in vain?

It is easier, of course, to identify this purblindness in other people : to condemn Jabez Balfour, for instance, for supposing that a gift of gold plate might be made to St. Paul's cathedral at the expense of his unfortunate investors.

Yet how often do our own faithful congregations esteem it better service to God to renew the heating system in church rather than devote the cost to famine relief? Those of us who have spent dreary hours in the sessions of church governing bodies, sessions in which the ability and goodness of many is wasted in the parching deserts of frustration, know how hard it is for any matter of more than immediate concern to find any place on the agenda. We can bicker affably for years over the reform of Canon Law (which most people will ignore), but find not a moment for slum landlords, doubtful patent medicines, or the hard core of unemployment. It is the curse of every church without exception — the Society of Friends would not wish to be called a church — that it spends so much time in introvert contemplation that little remains for serious consideration of other people's problems.

Micah, critical as he was of such an attitude, sets over against it a vision of world-mission and world fulfilment. We get no further than a series of "international gatherings" at which the same old voices proclaim the same old platitudes, the same old mussels are revealed clinging to the same old rocks.

NAHUM 1. 12–15; 2

89

ARMOURED DIVISIONS ON THE MOVE

THE BRITISH HAVE NEVER BEEN very good at "hate-poems"; they prefer to deride their enemies— "We'll hang out our washing on the Siegfried Line" — and to find amused rather than venomous epithets for them. ("Mounseers" or "fuzzy-wuzzies" or "Bolshies".) From the point of view of the persons concerned it is probably preferable to be treated as monstrous and terrifying, rather than trivial and entertaining, and the British technique may therefore be a highly subtle form of morale encouragement. But we are bad haters, with the weakness as well as the strength that this implies.

So we do not find it easy to understand a book like that of Nahum which is, simply, a continuous and hearty denunciation of the Assyrian nation and their capital city, Nineveh. Our reason for this is that we never in historical memory *really* suffered from any nation in the way, for example, the Jews of Warsaw suffered — or the people of Stalingrad — or the people of Hiroshima; the way the Bushmen suffered from the Bantu, or the aboriginals from the Tasmanian settlers. No prolonged and successful effort has been made to exterminate us — and that makes a good deal of difference to our attitude to others.

Now the Assyrians were the panzers of the ancient world. Their armoured chariots stormed across the frontiers and their siege trains demolished cities. They seemed quite irresistible until a combination of Medes and Babylonians overthrew their capital city of Nineveh after a three-years' siege.

This particular book, then, unique amongst prophets in that it makes no single solitary reference to *Jewish* moral failure, but only to judgement upon the enemy, is simply denunciation of the tyrant Assyria. It draws a picture of Herod out-Heroded, of the people who had so often stormed other people's cities seeing their own stripped and plundered. In chapter 3, verses 8 and 9 refer to the capture of the Egyptian city No-Aman by the Assyrian Asshur-banipal, but all the rest is a most stirring picture of the proud and wealthy city, whose symbol like that of Venice was the lion (chapter 2, verse 11), deserted by her defeated armies and herself sacked by the invader.

Has a writing of this kind any value for us, except as a comment on history? Does it help us to understand our world and ourselves any the better?

Only, perhaps, as a reminder as to just how much we have been insulated from the realities of history through the fact of our long immunity.

We can even look back on the War, most of us, without much sense of emotion. We crowd into a musical like *Blitz* which shows that war in the same sort of light that Thackeray threw on Waterloo — as a dramatic background to human affairs, as affecting their course, indeed, but never as overwhelming them. We need to try and understand what it would be like to have lost *every one* of our family in the gas-ovens, or to have been in Dresden when 170,000 died in the hell of British bombing. The city is perhaps man's greatest accomplishment in fellowship; the Bible itself hallows the whole idea of the city, ends with a heavenly city made perfect. Yet this symbol of neighbourly creativeness is also to be identified with the worst horrors of our fratricidal destructiveness. Our strength and our weakness are one — and perhaps the Book of Nahum can warn us of this terrible truth.

90

CRESCENDO—AND ALLEGRO

THIS PASSAGE IS A HYMN, PER-
haps written for use in the temple (before or after its restoration).
It contains therefore some musical directions. *Shigionoth,* for
instance, in verse 1, probably denotes "melodies of an irregular
character . . . reflecting sudden changes of emotion". Later on
in the chapter comes the word *"Selah",* which is uncertain in
translation but possibly means "Louder" — a direction either
to orchestra or to singers (compare the final verse). This is, in
fact, a hymn of the thundering "Onward, Christian soldiers"
sort, to be played with the loud pedal firmly down. Yet it has,
as such hymns often have not, two passages of deep pathos —
"in wrath, remember mercy" at the beginning, and verses 17
and 18 at the end. These two were taken by John Newton, ex-
captain of a slave ship, Rector of a City of London church,
writer of hymns, friend of William Wilberforce, as the text of
the sermon preached at the death of his adored wife.

If the first part of the hymn is a magnificent statement of the
power and glory of God, seen in geography no less than in
history, this final passage reminds us of the saints who have held
to their faith when all went against them. This is to discover
God in defeat and failure, the God who is despised and rejected,
but is still God undaunted. And there is about this moment of
disaster a mood, not of patient-Griselda endurance, but of actual
joy.

To endure the slings and arrows patiently is not in itself
uniquely Christian. The word "stoical" which we use of such
endurance is, after all, a reminder that the ancient philosophers
called "Stoics" not only taught but actively practised a philosophy of acceptance and fortitude. The histories of Greece and
Rome are full of stories of men — and women — who accepted
death and disaster without hope of future life, in the strength
of this belief. But it was never suggested that this endurance

should become actual joy. To die uncomplaining was one thing; to sing — as the Christian martyrs did in the arena — quite another.

Yet far too many Christians are content with the standard of the Stoics. Excluding the easy complainers — "I'm sure I don't know what I've done for God to treat me like this" — there are those who do indeed show patience in their troubles, but make that patience all too obvious to everybody else. There is a way of enduring trouble which is like showing your operation scars — everybody else is to know just how good you're being, and what a lot you have to put up with. "Isn't Mrs. C. wonderful? However she manages it, I don't know" — and you can be pretty sure that the pallid and virtuous face of Mrs. C. will wear a look of daily martyrdom.

But the real Christian spirit is so to endure our pains and griefs that other people simply don't know what is going on. Christ reminded us that those who fast should conceal the fact from their neighbours. Those who suffer may well remember, too, that useful prayer which reminds us that "pains in endurance are made twice as bad in description".

ZEPHANIAH 3

91

REVOLUTIONARY TORY

UNLIKE SOME OF HIS COL-
leagues, Zephaniah is, if his proudly stated pedigree in verse 1 of chapter 1 is to be believed, of the blood royal. But he is not, for that reason, a conservative. In fact, he has despaired of his own social class (chapter 3, verses 1–4) and turned instead to the poor (chapter 2, verse 3). He preaches revolution, that divine revolution which is the judgement of God on history (chapter 1, verses 14–18).

It affects every nation under heaven (chapter 2), but does not exclude his own. This is the opening theme of chapter 3, but in verse 9 it changes to a mood of tenderness. Not only, it suggests, will the dispersed and scattered Israelites be gathered home, but *all* the peoples of the world will know the one God and love and serve him. This new dispensation will be a social revolution as well, and after it the "poor but honest" will inherit the earth.

The end of the chapter is something of "pie in the sky by-and-by" — it encourages people to hold out and to wait for this consummation so devoutly to be wished.

Just how far is a book of this sort of spiritual value? What, after all, is it saying except this? — "There's going to be frightful trouble for everybody else, but never mind, you and I are going to be all right". This is a doctrine which is always cropping up in history and has its special appeal to the frustrated and inadequate. It makes them feel good — literally. So we find it, for instance, among Jehovah's Witnesses today. Now it is perfectly true that once people feel good they very often begin to behave better. They get rid of their sense of frustration and begin to act in a responsible way. But it doesn't necessarily make them responsible to more than their own immediate circle. It is as though the concern which should be exercised over the whole field of human contact (which is what we mean by "loving your neighbour") a concern which was before extremely dissipated and watery, becomes concentrated through its very limitation. It produces almost passionate loyalty within the immediate group and a scarcely less passionate antipathy outside it. This may enable those within it to get more meaning out of life, but it scarcely advances the progress of the world.

Nor does it do anything to set forward the kingdom of God, unless these minority groups are right (and they can't *all* be right about this) in believing that the kingdom of God is solely concerned with themselves and their promised future.

There is always a risk, then, that prophecy may be appropriated by those who need a crutch to help them through life — very much as prophecy's bastard descendant, popular astrology, is used by newspaper readers today. But it is, at the same time, a reminder of the dynamic and purpose of history. Events *are* significant, they *are* interrelated, they do form part of a pattern which makes sense to the observer, and he must, when he sees such a pattern in development, draw other people's attention to it, since it is a pattern still in the making of which the ultimate shape can be altered from moment to moment if only we care to try.

HAGGAI 1–2. 9

92

THE AFFLUENT SOCIETY

THE THEME OF THIS PARTICULAR book is simple. People bother about their own houses and their own comfort, but not about the temple, the house of God. This stands derelict, and nobody cares. Yet, all the time, because of their false sense of values, the social and economic life of the country is going to rack and ruin. It will only be when they come to see that their corporate and moral responsibility must come first that they will find the way to true prosperity. As Jesus put it, "Seek ye first the kingdom of God and his righteousness, and all these things (that is, material assets) will be added to you".

This is clearly much more than either a bribe for a church repair programme or the suggestion that such a programme will pay off in increased commercial prosperity ("give our movement a cheque : we'll beat the Communists, and the workers will work harder for the same money").

A nearer parallel, perhaps, would be the willingness of a community to spend money on public projects (and to be taxed to finance them) rather than use its resources for personal satisfactions.

> *"They shall be simple in their homes*
> *And splendid in their public ways."*

In practice, increasing affluence in a society seldom, if ever, appears to produce this result, as Galbraith points out in his book of the same name. It is in poorer societies that one finds a readiness to underwrite public expenditure, whether on architecture or on education. This may be partly due to the fact that, when individuals are rich, they tend to feel their dependence upon others lessened : indeed, sometimes suspicion and fear take its place. Instead of my neighbour being the person whose lawn-mower I borrow, he's the man who may want to borrow £100 from me. A society of rich individuals is apt, therefore, as examination of a really wealthy suburb will show, to be expressed in large houses concealed and indeed protected from each other by the highest of hedges, with a remarkable lack of communal facilities except for such non-individualist necessities as a golf club.

On the other hand, if I have few books of any use I can appreciate a public library : if I have no swimming pool of my own I want the one available to the public to be as large and clean as possible.

Now it is extremely hard for members of the affluent society to break through the inhibitions of their wealth. After all, so many of the possessions concerned are status symbols, overt tokens of the success of which the individual feels so proud. It is diffi-cult to substitute pride in the city bus-service for the self-satisfac-tion induced by visible ownership of a Rolls-Bentley : to be as happy to contribute, via taxation, for the purchase of a Leonardo da Vinci as to buy a Monet for oneself. But it is an attitude of mind that is not only Christian in itself but is also utterly essen-tial if our society is not to degenerate into a kind of gigantic suburban-sprawl, without dignity or centrality, without splen-dour and without glory.

ZECHARIAH
(summary)

93

THE POETS' PROPHET

THIS REALLY IS A DIFFICULT book. But it is a rewarding one. And it is more quoted in the New Testament than any other of the minor prophets; indeed, a great deal of the symbolism of the Revelation seems to be directly borrowed from it.

Those with time and patience to read through it slowly will find some splendid familiar individual passages (for instance, chapter 2, verses 10 and 11; chapter 4, verse 6; chapter 9, verse 9; chapter 11, verse 12; chapter 13, verse 6; chapter 14, verse 7).

But those who want to grasp some sort of connecting pattern will probably do better to take chapter 1, verses 1 to 13; chapter 3, verses 1 to 8; chapter 6, verses 1 to 13; the most beautiful of all passages (chapter 8, verses 4 to 8, and 19 to 23); and the last two verses of the last chapter.

Two themes then begin to emerge. The first is the use of poetic imagery. Poetry, it has been said, consists in taking two apparently quite unrelated objects — a broken heart and a bird on a branch, for instance — and making out of them a whole in which each illustrates the other. Sometimes the connection then becomes instantly obvious to the reader; sometimes it is so subtle, or so peculiar to the author, that only he can grasp it. Sometimes the connection may be simple in itself, but made difficult by the poet's handling of language. Zechariah is a poet, or a collection of poets — he looks out on a world so inter-penetrated with divinity that angels to him are common as apples — in which he resembles William Blake or Stanley Spencer. War and destruction trample down the earth like horse-men — for here are those same grim riders who reappear as the Four Horsemen of the Apocalypse. It is clear that Isael can never maintain its independence by military power, but it may become a spiritual kingdom relying not on walls, but on the Spirit of God. Zechariah dreams of a high priest who shall really be worthy of the name, of priest and king, ruling jointly like two shining lamps on the altar, and of justice and security for ever.

This is the second importance of the prophet — his recognition of holiness as something which is concerned with the total range of human life. He does not see the practice of piety as an end in itself, nor the worship of God as having meaning apart from its penetration of the everyday. To him the welfare of the old-age pensioner, the adventure playground of the city child, is as important as the integrity of the priest. The last two verses of the book emphasise this. We could paraphrase them by saying, "In that day the horns of buses shall sound to the glory of God . . . and the steam of every saucepan shall go up to his praise".

The mysterious staffs of chapter 11, verse 7 — Beauty and Bands — may stand for this twin character of the book, for imaginative poetry and practical application. All presentation of the gospel needs them both.

MALACHI: all, but note specially 1. 11; 2. 10; 3. 1–7, 16, 18; 4. 2, 5, 6

94

THE END OF THE LINE

THIS IS A LOVELY LITTLE BOOK, the last of the prophets. After it, though there were to be other writings of beauty and value (some of them are collected in the Apocrypha), the authentic voice is silent. And this book really tells us the reason. Religion had gone stale. People no longer cared about giving, but only about getting. The priesthood, the sons of Levi in chapter 2, are only concerned with what they can get out of it and charge heavily for every act of service. What is worse, no one is ashamed that this should be so, but they put up smoke-screens of words in self-justification. Nobody is even aware that anything is wrong or that their whole attitude to life is corrupted.

The three major notes of all traditional prophecy are therefore sounded, even though for the last time. First, the *"Day of the Lord"* — that's coming, all right, but it is coming with doom and judgement. Second, the *"Faithful Remnant"*. They, it is admitted, do exist (the end of chapter 3 and chapter 4), and they will be made manifest in the judgement. But chapter 1 (verse 11) is important, in that it suddenly widens the horizon. The Gentiles, the unwanted outcasts, are to take the place that faithless Israel has left empty.

Third, *"the Messiah"*. He is coming, but he will be heralded by a prophet, a new Elijah. When that forerunner appears, then indeed the king is coming back to his own.

It is, of course, these passages that Christians have always seen clearly fulfilled in the mission of John the Baptist.

What point has this book for us? Apart from the pathos of a voice that cries across the years of a man wistfully peering into darkness where only a sombre fire flickers, how does it "speak to our condition"?

It is, above all else, a warning against making religion cheap, against assuming that we can have it all our own way, cut to our fancy. Each of us needs to apply that warning against our knowledge of ourselves. It may suggest to us the possibility of a much greater generosity in the contribution of time and money made to the Church — or to human need. It may confront us (as in chapter 2, verse 14) with searching criticism of our behaviour to our own wife, or as in verse 10 of the same chapter, with our attitude in race relationships. It may involve our business and commercial ethics (chapter 3, verse 5); it may remind the ordained priest of his heavy responsibilities (chapter 2, verse 7).

In this respect, it anticipates the direct moral teaching of the prophet whose coming it foretells. Religion, says Malachi, is not a matter of intellectual discussion, nor yet of nominal allegiance. It is a matter of what you are — and this depends, in the end, on what you most value. No bad thing, indeed, that the Old Testament should end on such a note.